Behind the glory there is always a story

Table of Contents

This book is a heartfelt tribute to the incredible Eikonic Women who are fearlessly and authentically representing the female gender around the globe. I pray that your unwavering presence and power continues to inspire across generations. Additionally, I extend my deepest love to the ARC 2.0 women, who bring a refreshing breeze of encouragement into my life.

Kola my friend you are always remembered (S.I.P)

Introduction

When we were born, we were an empty book ready to be filled with all of life's expectations. As a child growing up, those expectations are normally extremely high, as we are oblivious to the many dangers that surround us. We were innocent and free, so we viewed life through the eyes of innocence. If you think back as you read this book, to your younger self, you will remember the many dreams and aspirations you had as a child. There was so much confidence that you were going to be exactly what you dreamt of becoming, and in this dream, there was no struggle, no roadblocks, or barriers to cross, just sheer bliss. I remember growing up being fascinated about flying in the sky, and so I told myself I was going to be an air hostess, wearing the fancy suits and pulling a luxurious suitcase, flying from one destination to the other, or better yet, I was going to be the pilot. This was just one of the many dreams that I had. The final outcome of either one was that I was going to be successful, and I am sure that I am not the only one.

I can see that little twinkle or smile in your eyes right now as you slyly remember that first dream of who you were going to become when you grew up. For some, maybe you hit the mark, and that's awesome!

However, for some of us, I bet you probably went completely in a different direction from the dream or what you spent all your time and money in UNI for, or you are right at that crossroads now. The truth, however, is that nothing prepares us for reality, and the reality is that just having the dream does not make it real. There is still a lot attached to that dream. Most of us are told what we should become by our parents, but the process of getting there is not detailed, or we don't get mentally or spiritually prepared for the journey that lies ahead. Yes, we may get the best schooling that money can buy, but I am sure that you would agree with me that the education system only prepares one to a certain level. Life's experiences and reality prepare us in a completely different way.

In this book, I speak about going from our lowest moments of life to knowing the true purpose of why God placed us here on this earth. At this moment, the individual that comes to my mind is one of the well-known characters in the Bible – Joseph, a.k.a 'The Dreamer.' Joseph had a journey that took him from being sold by his brothers, placed in a pit, and thrown into prison for something he did not do, to becoming the king's chief administrator of Egypt. Joseph was shown his future in a dream, a powerful vision of him being in a place of authority. But nowhere in that dream did he see the rough road he would have to pass to get there.

I remember a powerful sermon I have listened to multiple times by Dr. Darius Daniels titled 'I Didn't Know We Were Going This Way.' It made me pause and reflect on our journeys in life, particularly when it comes to God's guidance. Dr. Daniels highlighted something that deeply resonated with me - the idea that even though a shorter route may exist to reach our destination, God might take us on a longer, unexpected path. Why? Because there are valuable lessons, personal and spiritual growth waiting for us along the way.

As I sit here, writing these words, I can't help but smile. The beauty of being on a journey with God is that He knows what's best for us, even when we can't see it. He takes us on routes we didn't anticipate, sometimes longer ones, even when there may have been a shortcut available. But His plans are purposeful, aiming to shape our character and equip us with the attributes we need to thrive in our positions.

It's important to remember that where you find yourself right now may be vastly different from where you imagined or even believed you were destined to be. But here's the reassuring truth: God doesn't make mistakes. He is intentional in every step He leads us through. Sometimes, the path ahead may appear bleak or uncertain, causing us to question God's intentions. But in those moments, let's hold onto the faith that He sees the bigger picture, even when we can't fully comprehend it.

Think about it, how many times have you taken the supposed shortcut, opted for the cheaper option, only to realise that it ended up costing you more time and effort in the end?

We've all been there, my sisters…Picture this: you're driving and encounter heavy traffic. Amidst the frustration, you think, "I know another route!" So, you take that detour, only to find out that the traffic on that road is even worse. Possibly you have been in a battle of wills with the Satnav or Waze, questioning their choice of a longer route? And then, against your instincts, you decide to go your own way, the familiar shorter path, only to see that dreaded red line appear on the screen. Oh, the frustrating realisation or the rhetorical question – 'why didn't I just follow the Satnavs instructions? You know why? It is because at times we get carried away with what is immediately in front of us rather than the destination.

But here's my encouragement to you, my sweet sister, don't give up or allow yourself to be discouraged. Trust in God to be your navigator. He sees the bigger picture and knows the routes that you should take. He's got you, my dear. In those moments when it feels like you have to choose between your instincts and the guidance from above, remember that God's direction often leads us on the path of growth and blessings.

So, hold on tight. Trust in God's guidance, even if His chosen route seems longer or unfamiliar at first. Embrace the journey with faith and patience, knowing that He is leading you towards something greater. Your detours and unexpected roads are part of a grand plan, moulding you into the incredible woman you were always meant to be. Keep your head held high and trust that God's navigation will ultimately guide you to your destination, even if the path may differ from what you initially imagined.

As we continue on our individual journeys of faith, personal growth and vision let's embrace the unexpected routes, the detours, and the winding paths. Let's trust that God's guidance is purposeful and that He is preparing us for greatness. So, keep your head up, and know that your desires will come to fruition in their own divine timing. Together, let's celebrate the beauty of the unexpected and embrace the journey with open hearts and unwavering faith. With anticipation for our future conversations and shared growth. I felt led to write this book as my journey has been one similar to Joseph. I am now living my purpose, but it took me through a path that I never anticipated, and halfway on this journey, I began to give up and no longer believed that my dream was possible. I did not even believe in it or myself anymore. Debt, depression, and abuse are some of the many experiences that I had; however, one thing is for certain, I lost my identity along the way but also found out WHO I TRULY WAS, (sometimes we operate under a mistaken identity – we will get into that a bit later). My strengths and abilities, but more importantly my purpose. You see, I made the decision to turn my pain into a passion. I learned through it all not to be bitter but to get better, to not use the challenges as an excuse to give up, but instead a reason to fight. I am grateful for my past and who it has enabled me to become.

Today, so many women have given up on themselves and the life that they desired because of the journey they are on or have already gone on and the original destination seems no longer to be in sight, which then opens the door to weariness, dismay, and a loss of hope. There are many women, maybe even you who are reading this right now, that are currently ill or going through a place of anxiety and doubt, all due to the effects of what could have or should have been.

When hope is delayed or lost, it can deeply affect the hearts of individuals – as the great book tells us in Proverbs 13:12, "Hope deferred makes the heart sick." You may even be experiencing despair, depression, and a loss of motivation, believing that your dreams are unattainable after facing difficult circumstances.

It is for this very reason that I have penned this book, to remind you that even in the midst of challenging cards dealt by life, there is always hope. As long as you are alive, your purpose remains alive too, waiting to be reignited.

So, sis, let us hit this journey together and create not only your desired life but a life that you deserve x

- *It's not a mess but an incomplete message*
- *Perspective shift*
- *Be Still*
- *I almost killed that girl!*

The Eikonic Woman

CHAPTER ONE

The Eikonic Woman

"I would like to be known as an intelligent woman, a courageous woman, a loving woman, a woman who teaches by being."

MAYA ANGELOU

Most people are only aware or have recognition of the word "icon" and so may be puzzled by the spelling used in this book ("Eikon"). However, let's take a look at the etymology of the word "icon". The word "icon", according to Wikipedia, means 'a person or thing widely admired especially for having great influence or significance in a particular sphere.' It stems from the ancient Greek word "*eikenai*" ("Eikon"), meaning image or representation. I thought let me get that out there before I introduce to you the "Eikonic woman."The Eikonic Woman, my dear sister, is a force to be reckoned with. She embodies the essence of bold influence and spiritual fortitude. She is authentically herself, radiating wisdom, ambition, and humility. As a woman of prominence, she carries herself with value and authority, nurturing her innate creativity and embracing her authentic self. She fearlessly takes risks, not only building her home but also uplifting and empowering those around her whilst cultivating a balanced and purpose filled life.

What sets her apart is her selflessness and courage. She understands the power of showing up, not just for herself, but as a representative of something greater. And oh, my darling, she is truly beautiful, inside and out. Her beauty shines through her actions, her words, and the way she embraces life's challenges with grace and resilience.

You see, the Eikonic Woman is so much more than just a label or a title. She is a symbol of collective strength and growth. She constantly strives to better herself while lifting others along the way. She believes in the power of community and shared success, knowing that when women come together, amazing things happen.

So, my dear Eikonic Woman, continue to be bold in your influence, spiritually equipped in your journey, and authentic in all that you do. Embrace your wisdom, ambition, and humility, for they are the pillars that hold your greatness. Keep taking risks, building not just a home but a tribe of strong and empowered women. Show up, always, and represent all that is beautiful, courageous, successful, and transformative in this world.

When I started writing this book, I thought to myself, 'there are so many of these diamonds out there, hidden under the dust of all that is happening around them, and now it is time to dig them out, it is time to dust off those gems so that they can shine.

Yes, you, I am speaking about and to you!

My Eikonic sister, for too long you have been buried under the rubble of life, wondering if change is going to come. I am here to tell you that your change is already within. The fact that dirt is covering the diamond doesn't mean that it has lost its value – now stop and think about that for a hot minute.

So, this is my take on it all...

> *Your life – It's not a mess but*
> *an incomplete message.*

The MESSage

In a world obsessed with perfection and completed narratives, we often find ourselves questioning the messiness of our lives. We find ourselves going through the MESS-AGE. We strive to paint a picture of flawlessness, afraid to reveal the incomplete aspects of our stories. But what if we shifted our perspective? What if we started seeing our lives not as a mess, but as an unfinished message waiting to be unveiled? In this section, we explore the transformative power of embracing incompleteness and how it can lead to growth, resilience, and unbounded possibilities.

So, let's then firstly look at redefining messiness and embracing imperfections. Redefining messiness is about shifting our perception and embracing the inherent imperfections and unpredictability of life. It means letting go of the traditional notion that an orderly and flawlessly executed existence is the ultimate goal. Instead, we recognise that messiness is an integral part of growth, creativity, and resilience. By reframing our understanding of messiness, we open ourselves up to new possibilities, learn to navigate uncertainty with courage, and find beauty in the imperfect moments. It is through this process of redefinition that we discover the power and freedom that comes from embracing the messiness and embracing the fullness of life.

In today's society, as women, we have to redefine the concept of messiness in our lives. No longer should you be confined by societal expectations of perfection and flawlessness; embracing the messiness is and should be a sign of individuality and strength. You need to break free from the idea that your life should follow a linear and predictable path, instead of choosing to navigate the twists and turns with resilience and grace. Instead of trying to be a one size fits all woman, where you are trying to be like everyone else, why not rewrite the narrative, see your imperfections as opportunities for growth and self-discovery.

By redefining messiness, you are finding empowerment in your unique journey and embracing the beauty that emerges from the unfinished and imperfect aspects of your life.

Overcoming society's unrealistic expectations of perfection is a powerful journey that many women have now started to embark upon. Society often imposes unattainable standards of beauty, success, and behaviour on us as women, leading to many having feelings of inadequacy and self-doubt. However, now is the time for you to challenge and dismantle these expectations. It's time to embrace your unique qualities and redefine what it means to be beautiful, successful, and fulfilled. By rejecting the pursuit of perfection and instead the pursuit of happiness, you are embracing self-acceptance, self-love, and self-care.

It's time to prioritise your mental and emotional well-being, celebrate your strengths, and value your authentic selves. I got to the point where I became tired of the world's expectations and decided to allow my authentic self to shine. Anyone that knows or meets me knows that I keep it 100% real. Because here's the thing, overcoming society's unrealistic expectations will allow you to be and show up more authentic in the world, as there is a sense of freedom that comes from embracing the beauty within imperfections and reshaping the narrative from messy to an incomplete message.

From my experiences, some of which I will share with you shortly, I have come to realise that recognising the dynamic nature of our lives and experiences is a powerful tool and at times is the very thing that leads us to our purpose. Recognising the dynamism of our lives means understanding that we are constantly evolving and experiencing different phases, circumstances, and opportunities. It involves accepting that mistakes and setbacks are valuable lessons that contribute to our growth and personal development. Rather than seeing mistakes as failures, we can view them as opportunities to identify areas that need improvement and work on them so that the message can be developed.

To illustrate this, imagine going down a road you've never been before and accidentally falling into a ditch. It may be painful and unfortunate, but now you're aware of the existence and location of the ditch. This knowledge and experience will enable you to navigate the road more effectively and even help others avoid the same pitfall.

Ultimately, recognising the dynamic nature of our lives and experiences allows us to embrace change, learn from our journey, and live with a greater sense of authenticity and fulfilment. It enables us to embrace the messiness and uncertainties, knowing that they are part of our unique and ever-evolving story. Anyone who knows me would know that I strongly resent the idea or notion that a "messy" life equates to failure. I believe that no one, and I mean no one, should be written off. By challenging the idea that a messy life equals failure, we begin to embrace the beauty and growth that can come from navigating through life's struggles. Instead of viewing setbacks, mistakes, and detours as signs of failure, we start seeing them as opportunities for learning, resilience, and personal growth.

Let me share a truth with you - a messy life isn't a sign of failure but rather a testament to a life lived boldly. It's the result of taking risks, exploring new paths, and challenging the status quo. It means embracing authenticity and exhibiting courage in every step we take. So, let's reframe our perspective, shall we? Instead of seeing our messy lives as something to be ashamed of, let's start valuing the lessons we've learned from our imperfections. (**Take a moment to reflect and evaluate those moments you have experienced and analyse what strength, insight or understanding you have gained?**)

Each stumble and every obstacle we've overcome has made us stronger. By challenging the notion that mess equates to failure, we open up space for self-compassion, acceptance, and growth. If you are wondering if I know what I am talking about, trust me, I can relate to your feelings. There have been moments when I felt my life was so messy that I questioned my very purpose on this earth. I saw myself as a worn-out car, beyond repair. But you know what? Even those cars can be scrapped and still earn something from it. Yet, I did not believe that anything good could come out of me. It reminded me of the question asked about Jesus in the Bible, "Can anything good come out of Nazareth?" But here's the beauty of it all: we don't have to see mess as the end. In fact, that belief is what inspired me to stand firmly in my conviction that as long as there is life, there is hope. No one's life deserves to be seen as a complete failure. The fact that you may be at a certain age and haven't achieved certain things does not mean that it's no longer possible. It's never too late for growth, for transformation, and for the pursuit of our dreams.

So, remember that your 'messy life' is a tapestry of experiences that have shaped you into the remarkable woman you are today. Embrace it, learn from it, and believe in the infinite possibilities that lie ahead. Your journey is filled with hope and potential, and together, we can inspire and uplift each other as we navigate through the 'messiness' of life.

Shift your perspective

A powerful skill or tool that I have leaned on and utilised over the years is the ability to shift my perspective. This has helped keep me from wallowing in self-pity, wearing myself out by fighting every single battle that showed up, seeing some issues bigger than they really are, and the consequences of this tends to be anxiety, stress, depression, amongst so many other things.

So, what do I mean by shifting your perspective?

I mean giving yourself the opportunity to look at things through a different lens. The shifting of perspective refers to the ability to step back from your viewpoint and see a situation from different angles. It involves questioning your own beliefs, biases, and assumptions and opening yourself up to new possibilities and interpretations. Here's the thing, by shifting your perspective, you gain a broader understanding of a situation and can make more informed decisions with clarity. When you shift your perspective, you release yourself from the limitations of your viewpoint and begin to examine things objectively. This process allows you to consider alternative viewpoints, challenge ingrained patterns of thinking, and explore different solutions to problems. The beauty of shifting your perspective is that it allows you to cultivate a mindset that is open, flexible, and receptive to new ideas and experiences.

It enables you to break free from rigid thinking and embrace a more expansive and inclusive way of understanding the world. This practice of shifting perspective is a powerful practice that I believe everyone should utilise, but it is particularly beneficial in overcoming challenges as a woman.

Just in case you are asking or wondering why, let us dig a little deeper.

Women, more than men, fight numerous mental battles. Don't get me wrong, men do too, but women face a tumult of ongoing mental pressures.

Here are some common ones faced that you may be able to relate to or know someone who can:

1. **Societal expectations**: Women often face pressure to fulfil multiple roles and meet societal expectations, such as being a caregiver, homemaker, and breadwinner simultaneously. These expectations can lead to feelings of stress, overwhelm, and burnout.

2. **Body image and appearance**: Society's emphasis on physical appearance can put significant pressure on women to achieve a certain standard of beauty. This can lead to body image issues, low self-esteem, suicidal tendencies, depression, and eating disorders.

3. **Work-life balance**: Balancing work and personal life can be challenging for women, especially when societal expectations and workplace norms don't always support flexibility and work-life integration. This pressure to excel professionally while maintaining personal responsibilities can contribute to stress and anxiety.

4. **Gender inequality**: Women may face discrimination, sexism, and unequal treatment in various aspects of life, including education, employment, and healthcare. These experiences can take a toll on mental health, leading to feelings of frustration, anger, and self-doubt.

5. **Domestic responsibilities**: Women often shoulder a significant portion of domestic responsibilities, including housework and caregiving. This added burden can lead to feelings of exhaustion, resentment, and a lack of time for self-care.

6. **Gender-based violence**: Women may face the fear and trauma of experiencing gender-based violence, including domestic violence, sexual harassment, and assault. These experiences can have severe mental health consequences, such as post-traumatic stress disorder (PTSD) and anxiety disorders.

7. **Past Traumas**: from rape, child abuse, grooming, and molestation. All of which cause an ongoing life of traumatic stress.

This list could go on and on.

Now why am I highlighting these points? Well, with this barrage of bullets warring against the mind and the additional issues of daily life, it is imperative that as a woman, we create mechanisms to help us not only protect our sanity but also enable us to have the ability to remain resilient and strong during the chaotic moments. To look at situations as they come to us with a mindset that enables us to find solutions instead of dwelling on the problem and digging an even bigger hole than what was already there. It's important to note that the impact of these pressures can vary for each individual, and not all women may experience them in the same way. However, the main point I am highlighting here is that regardless of the situation and how we experience them as women, it is imperative that we think strategically and take tactical actions. The only way we can do this is by shifting perspective, or going from the biblical angle of 'renewing our minds daily.'

Ah, let's take a look at this age-old question: Is the glass half full or half empty?

It's an intriguing concept that speaks to our perception and mindset. The way we view that glass can reveal a lot about our outlook on life.

Now, there's no denying that we all face challenges and setbacks along our journeys. In those moments, it can be all too easy to see the glass as half empty – focusing on what's lacking or what hasn't gone as planned. It's a perspective that can cast a shadow over our lives and dampen our spirits. But here's the beautiful truth, sis: You have the power to shift that perspective. You can choose to see the glass as half full. You can choose to focus on the abundance and the possibilities that lie before you.

By embracing an optimistic outlook, you nourish your spirit and infuse your life with a sense of hope and resilience. Seeing the glass as half full means recognising the blessings and opportunities that surround you, even amidst challenges. It's about finding gratitude for what you have, celebrating your achievements, and recognising the potential for growth in every situation.

Now, let me tell you a little secret: Seeing the glass as half full doesn't mean you ignore or deny the difficulties you may face. It's about acknowledging the reality of the situation while choosing to focus on what you can control and the positive aspects within your reach. It's about choosing a mindset of abundance and embodying the belief that you have the power to create a life filled with joy, fulfilment, and success. Remember, shifting your perspective takes practice and self-compassion. It's a journey of self-discovery and growth. But every step you take toward embracing a half-full mindset brings you closer to unlocking your true potential and living a life that is rich with purpose and possibility.

Shifting your perspective can be a powerful tool for personal growth and transformation. Here are a few strategies you can try to change your perspective:

1. **Practice Mindfulness**: Take a moment to pause, breathe, and tune into the present moment. Mindfulness helps you shift your focus away from racing thoughts and worries and cultivates a sense of calm. By grounding yourself in the present, you can gain a fresh perspective on your thoughts, emotions, and circumstances.

2. **Seek New Experiences**: Stepping out of your comfort zone and embracing new experiences can broaden your horizons and shift your perspective. Travel to new places, try new activities, or immerse yourself in unfamiliar cultures. These experiences can challenge your assumptions and open your mind to different ways of thinking and living.

3. **Engage in Self-Reflection**: Set aside time for self-reflection, whether through journaling, meditation, or simply sitting quietly with your thoughts. Reflect on your beliefs, values, and experiences. Ask yourself thought-provoking questions to gain deeper insights into your thoughts and behaviours. This introspection can help you identify patterns and biases that may be limiting your perspective.

4. **Practice Gratitude**: Cultivating a gratitude practice can transform your mindset and shift your perspective to focus on the positive aspects of your life. Take a few moments each day to acknowledge and appreciate the things you are grateful for. This practice can shift your attention away from negativity and help you see the blessings and opportunities that surround you.

5. **Seek Different Perspectives**: Engage in conversations with people who have different backgrounds, beliefs, and experiences than your own. Actively listen to their viewpoints with an open mind and try to understand their perspectives. This can challenge your own preconceived notions and expand your understanding of the world.

6. **Challenge Negative Thoughts**: Be aware of negative thought patterns that may be skewing your perspective. When you catch yourself engaging in negative self-talk or catastrophising, consciously challenge those thoughts. Reframe negative experiences by focusing on the lessons or opportunities they may bring. Replace negative thoughts with positive and empowering affirmations. A basic analogy that I use in this instance is a bin. The use of a bin is to put rubbish - yes? So any rubbish thought operating in my mind or anything that was said or done dumped. You know why that is? Because your brain is not a rubbish bin, so why would you allow rubbish to be dumped there, it will slowly begin to stink.

7. **Pray**: Prayer changes things - Proverbs 3:5-6 states "Trust in the Lord with all of your heart and lean not on your own understanding, in all your ways, acknowledge Him and He shall direct your path." Prayer allows you to bring your

worries and challenges to the Lord, laying them at the master's feet so you don't have to be burdened with the cares of this world. The fact that the Bible tells us in Romans 12:1-2 to renew our minds daily signifies that the Lord knows that we will be challenged daily by not only external influences but also our own intrusive thoughts.

If you are still wondering why having the right mindset is important for you as a woman, especially a woman who is planning to turn her ideas into a business, well stop for a minute and think about your self-worth. If you are someone who is battling with not knowing who you are and what you are worth, then you will never step up to the position of being and charging clients what you are truly worth. This I will not elaborate on here but will take a deeper dive into when we speak about identity.

Remember, changing your perspective and working on your mindset is a journey that requires practice and self-compassion. Be patient with yourself and celebrate every small step forward. Embrace the growth that comes from exploring new viewpoints and challenging your own beliefs. You have the power to shape your perspective and create a life filled with joy, growth, and authenticity

Ladies your mindset is a potent force, capable of shaping your reality. Speaking about minds, let's take a deeper stroll down the mindset lane. Most of you reading this book will either already be in business or interested in starting a business or excelling in your career in the near future. When it comes to starting out in business or growth in general, having the right mindset is of utmost importance. The journey of progression is often filled with challenges, uncertainties, and setbacks, and it requires a positive and resilient mindset to overcome these obstacles. A growth mindset is essential, as it allows you to embrace learning, adapt to changing circumstances, and view failures as opportunities for growth. Additionally, a focused and determined mindset will help you stay motivated and committed to your goals, even in the face of adversity. It enables us to make strategic decisions, take calculated risks, and persistently work towards our vision. Moreover, having an optimistic and solution-oriented mindset helps us navigate the ups and downs of personal and business life with grace and flexibility. With the right mindset, you can overcome challenges, seize opportunities, and ultimately create success and fulfilment in your ventures – we will speak more on this in a further chapter.

> *Ladies your mindset is a potent force, capable of shaping your reality*

Having a shift in perspective is just one way that you can train your mind in the game of business, in fact, life in general. Therefore, training your mind to have the right mindset is crucial. Our mindset shapes our thoughts, beliefs, attitudes, and actions, which ultimately determine our level of success and fulfilment.

Let me share a few reasons based on my experience why a positive and empowering mindset is important:

Resilience

A strong mindset helps us bounce back from setbacks, challenges, and failures. It allows us to view obstacles as opportunities for growth and learning, rather than insurmountable barriers. With a resilient mindset, we can persevere through difficult times and maintain our motivation and focus.

Growth and Learning

A growth mindset emphasises the belief that abilities and skills can be developed through dedication and effort. By embracing a growth mindset, we open ourselves up to continuous learning, improvement, and adaptation. This mindset encourages exploration, creativity, and innovation, which are vital in the game of business.

Confidence

A positive mindset cultivates self-confidence and self-belief, which are essential for success. When we believe in ourselves and our abilities, we are more likely to take risks, embrace challenges, and seize opportunities. Confidence inspires others, attracts support and collaboration, and helps us navigate uncertainty with poise and determination.

Goal Setting and Achievement

Having a focused and goal-oriented mindset enables us to set meaningful goals and work towards their fulfilment. With a clear vision and a positive mindset, we can develop effective strategies, overcome obstacles, and stay committed to achieving our desired outcomes. Our mindset influences our motivation, perseverance, and discipline to pursue our goals relentlessly.

Relationships and Networking

A positive mindset fosters healthy and positive relationships with others. By maintaining an optimistic and collaborative mindset, we can attract supportive mentors, peers, and customers. A positive mindset also enables us to build strong networks, collaborate effectively, and inspire others with our enthusiasm and vision.

Well-being and Fulfilment

Ultimately, having the right mindset contributes to our overall well-being and fulfilment. It allows us to cultivate gratitude, embrace optimism, and find joy and satisfaction in the journey towards success. By focusing on positive thoughts and emotions, we can reduce stress, increase resilience, and lead a more fulfilling and balanced life.

Remember, building the right mindset is an ongoing practice. It requires self-awareness, reflection, and intentional effort to reframe negative thoughts, challenge limiting beliefs, and cultivate positive habits. By consistently nourishing a positive mindset, we can unlock our full potential and create success and fulfilment in both the game of business and life.

Be Still

Another weapon I believe an Eikonic woman would need to use and cultivate in order to be and remain victorious is the art or ability to be still.

What do I mean by "be still"?

I mean being still and sometimes silent when situations arise, maintaining a sense of calm, composure, and inner peace in the face of adversity. It involves refraining from reactive or impulsive behaviours and instead choosing to respond in a thoughtful and measured manner. There are several reasons why being still in challenging situations is important. When we take the time to be still, it opens the door to clarity and perspective. In those moments, we create space to step back, objectively assess the situation, and consider various options and solutions. By resisting the urge to react impulsively, we can make more informed and rational decisions that can lead to better outcomes. Additionally, being still allows us to regulate our emotions effectively. When faced with difficult situations, we may experience anger, fear, or frustration. By pausing and acknowledging these emotions, we can process them before responding. This prevents our emotions from controlling our actions and empowers us to respond in a composed and rational manner. Furthermore, being still plays a vital role in problem-solving. Bad situations often require us to engage our problem-solving abilities to navigate through them successfully. By being still, we can assess the situation, gather information, and explore potential solutions with a clear and focused mindset. This approach increases our chances of finding effective solutions that lead to positive outcomes.

In challenging circumstances, effective communication becomes even more crucial. Taking a moment to be still allows us to gather our thoughts and choose our words wisely. It helps us express ourselves clearly and constructively, improving our ability to resolve conflicts, diffuse tension, and build positive relationships.

Lastly, being still prioritises our own well-being and self-care. It provides us with an opportunity to assess our needs, set boundaries, and practice self-care strategies that support our emotional and mental well-being. By recognising when and how to protect ourselves from further harm, being still empowers us to prioritise our own well-being in challenging situations. Remember, embracing stillness can empower you to navigate challenging circumstances with grace and resilience. Take the time to be still, and you'll unlock a wealth of clarity, emotional regulation, problem-solving capabilities, effective communication, and self-care practices. Here's to your continued growth and success as you embrace the power of stillness in your personal and entrepreneurial journey!

In summary, being still when bad situations arise is important because it allows us to approach challenges with clarity, emotional regulation, problem-solving skills, effective communication, and a focus on self-care. This practice empowers us to make better decisions, maintain our composure, and navigate difficult circumstances with resilience and grace.

Ladies, I am sure you would agree with me that life has a way of throwing unexpected challenges our way. It can sometimes feel like we are caught in a whirlwind of chaos, with no respite in sight. But in the midst of these storms, there is a powerful tool that we can wield - the art of being still.

Psalm 46:10 ESV
"Be still, and know that I am God.
I will be exalted among the nations,
I will be exalted in the earth!"

In Psalm 46, the author finds solace in God as their refuge and strength amid turmoil. The call to "Be still and know that I am God" prompts reflection on God's control in our lives. Taking time to connect with faith brings peace in chaos, gratitude in trials, and strength through prayer. Being still may be challenging, yet it enriches us as we acknowledge God's presence and guidance in the midst of chaos.

Picture this: you're faced with a mountain of obstacles, uncertainties, and setbacks. Your mind is racing, your heart is heavy, and it seems impossible to find a sense of grounding amidst the turmoil. This is when stillness becomes your beacon of light, guiding you through the darkest of times. Being still doesn't mean being stagnant or passive; it is an active choice to pause, breathe, and find solace within. It is in these moments of quiet reflection that we can tap into our inner strength, gather our thoughts, gain clarity amidst the chaos and allow our ears to be sensitive to the voice of the Holy Spirit. When challenges arise, it's easy to get swept up in the whirlpool of emotions and external pressures. We may feel overwhelmed, anxious, or even tempted to give up. But my ladies, this is when being still becomes an act of rebellion, a declaration of our resilience, a refusal to quit.

Embracing stillness allows us to create a space for self-care, self-compassion, and self-discovery. It's where we can detach ourselves from the noise and reconnect with our inner truth. In the midst of challenges, stillness becomes our safe haven, a sanctuary where we can nurture our soul and find peace amidst the storm. But don't be mistaken, stillness does not banish challenges or make them disappear. Instead, it equips us with the clarity and strength we need to navigate them with grace and resilience. It provides us with the perspective to see obstacles as opportunities for growth and transformation.

So, in the face of adversity, let us remember the power of being still. Take a moment to close your eyes, breathe deeply, and release the tension that lingers within you. Allow yourself to feel grounded, present, and supported by your inner wisdom and the collective strength of women who have walked similar paths. As you move through the challenges that life presents, embrace stillness as your secret weapon. Let it be the guiding force that helps you maintain balance, find clarity, and rise above the storm. Remember, it is through the stillness that we uncover our true power and emerge as strong, resilient, and unstoppable. Therefore, it is time to channel that stillness in order to reveal the inner strength that stillness brings.

Let me take a moment to share a bit of my personal story with you because I truly believe it will help you understand the importance of what I've already shared and how it can pave the way for you to transform your pain into profit and create the life you truly desire and deserve. You see, I've been where you are. I've experienced those moments of uncertainty, doubt, and even pain. But through it all, I've discovered that embracing the challenges and setbacks is what truly propels us forward on our journey to success.

I remember a time when I faced a major setback in my career. It felt like everything was falling apart, and I didn't know how to move forward. But instead of giving up, I decided to be still and reflect on what I really wanted. I took the time to tap into my inner strength, assess my skills and passions, and ultimately chart a new course that aligned with my true desires. And you know what? That moment of stillness, of taking a breath and really listening to my inner voice, became the turning point in my life. It was the catalyst for transforming my pain into profit and creating a life that I not only desired but truly deserved.

> *Remember, it is through the stillness that we uncover our true power and emerge as strong, resilient, and unstoppable.*

That's why I'm so passionate about sharing this message with you today. I want you to know that you have within you the power to overcome any obstacle, to rise above the challenges, and to create a life that is truly fulfilling and aligned with your deepest desires.

So, take a moment to be still. Reflect on your journey, embrace the lessons from your past, and allow them to guide you towards a future filled with abundance and success. You deserve nothing less.

I almost killed that girl!

As she sits at her black glass desk in the tiny but very comfy eye-catching turquoise blue and white office located in her back garden, she gazes out the window located in front of her, which gives a full view of the back of her house. There is the refreshing smell of greenery as the sun streams in, and she starts to reflect on her journey.

"How did I get here?" The success, despite the many hurdles running through her mind, like pop-up images on a big cinema screen, it had not been an easy ride that took her to this moment. The trophies, pictures, her books, and those of clients sitting on the shelves in the unit behind her gives a brief glimpse into what she has been able to accomplish. A deep feeling of gratitude as a tear begins to roll down her right cheek, looking at the house in front of her and remembering the day a bailiff stood outside the door of her house where she once lived, trying to get in to take away the few possessions both she and the two beautiful children she had at the time had left. How did I get from there to this? Now being the owner and Landlord of that very house she nearly got evicted from – a few moments of becoming homeless. The question kept coming back to her in such a profound way, the only answer she could conjure up was God, hard work, and belief. If you were there within earshot as she asked this question aloud, I am sure that you would have a few questions of your own to ask: Where is there? Where was she coming from? What were some of the things she went through?

You see, this lady is me, Michelle Watson, a bestselling author, Performance mentor, Multi-award winning international speaker, Deacon, Podcast host and the Founder of The Eikonic Women. She is also the proud mother of three beautiful children and a wife to one of the best men in the world. However, despite the many accolades that I now have, there is a story and journey behind it all. Things did not come about easily, and maybe as you are reading this right now, you can relate.

For a long time, I was lost, unsure of where my life would be and the purpose of me being here on this earth. For some who know me but do not know my story, they may be thinking - really?

Well, join me in the year 2004, and here you see me in a very challenging situation. I am just coming in from a night of dinner and cinema with my friends, with a banging headache and my heart pounding so hard it feels as though my chest is about to burst. And if you are wondering, no, my headache is not from drinking. I am standing with my back pressed firmly against the locked white door in my small magnolia-painted bathroom. The white porcelain bath is to my right, the toilet is to the front on my left, and the face basin immediately in front of me below a window that I believe is too massive for a bathroom. The distinct smell of bleach is playing havoc on my nostrils, but I could never clean my bathroom without a lot of bleach. I just wish it could help to clean all the muck that is in my life right now.

'Oh no, is that him?' I jump as I hear a sound and crouch sideways to put my ears close up to the door. I know he's not gone and is still out there waiting for me to come out. Why am I here again? Over and over, I tell myself, 'No more – it is not going to happen again,' but somehow, I still end up finding myself in the same or worse position. Nicky keeps telling me, but I never listen: "Michelle, you don't see that he is going to kill you. Are you going to remain like this forever?"

"You refuse to tell your family, and all you do is get up and write in journals as if you can write it all away. If you are not careful, it won't be your journal that will be written into, it will be your eulogy that we will be writing."

Nicky is a close friend of mine; you know, Nicky is a close friend of mine; you know, the ones that tell it like it is with her hint of Jamaican accent. She just does not understand. I cannot just leave and become a divorcee in my early twenties. How can someone who once looked at you with so much love and compassion now look at you with such disgust and hate? How can the hands that once made you tingle with life now inflict so much pain? How could the smile that once made you melt now just curdle your blood, and the words that made your heart skip a beat now change to so much filth that you feel like the scum of the earth? Dr. Jekyll and Mr. Hyde, you know the character with two personalities, and to be going through this with him for nearly five years has slowly destroyed me.

The shame of telling my family is too much. To tell anyone would be too much. Nicky only knew because she had seen the marks and heard the sounds. All I wanted was one night out with my friends. I had just been told that I had a tumour behind my left ear, resting on my nerve, and there was a 99% chance that the left side of my face would be paralysed after the operation. I just wanted to be with my friends, something that I had also been deprived of, and as you can guess, he was not happy about that. So here I am with my head spinning like a butterfly and my bruises stinging like a bee, as if I had just gone through a few rounds in the ring with the great Muhammad Ali.

Oh no, the kids! I must get out. I cannot let him take the kids.

Have you ever had to make a decision - a very big decision? Well, that night I decided not to just face whatever was coming to me by stepping out of the bathroom, but I also stepped out of the marriage. I would love to tell you that it was easy, but it was not, as I found it hard to tell my family. I felt ashamed - ashamed that I had allowed myself to be someone else's punching bag. So I spent most days staying at my friend's house.

Have you ever played the board game Snakes and Ladders? You've shaken your dice and gotten the biggest numbers, two sixes, and you happily move up your spaces. Oh boy, you are excited because you end up also getting a bonus to climb higher by going up the ladder, only to land on the mouth of a snake which takes you all the way back down to its tail, at the very beginning of the board. Have you ever felt like that? As if you are running through hoops but getting nowhere? Well, 4 months later, you would see me stepping into yet another small room: brilliant white-painted walls, a dark brown sofa to my right, a desk and chair to my left, and a massive plant standing in the corner. There was a lovely smell of summer breeze vanilla air freshener, and the room was brightly lit by the see-through windows going down the right side of the wall. But somehow, I seemed to have darkness all around me. There he is. Tall, dark, and handsome. He could be a basketball player, apart from the glasses perched on the edge of his nose that made him look a bit like a geek.

"Hello Michelle, do come in and take a seat. Is it alright for me to call you Michelle?" he said with his bright yet soft-spoken voice. "Yes," I replied, hardly being able to open my mouth.

"Yes, Michelle, whatever makes you comfortable. So, I have gone through your notes and the forms you have filled out, but can I hear from you what really brings you here today?"

My hands began to shake, and the erratic, cracked voice that began to speak sounded nothing like me.

"I feel like I am going mad, and I know they think I am going mad, but I know he is following me."

"Michelle, who is following you?"

"My ex. He is following me wherever I go. I will go to the store and he's there. I leave my house to go to work, and when I return, all my clothes are missing from the closet. Another time, it was my purse and passport. I go to my friend's house, and all four of my tyres get slashed outside her house. That is not a coincidence. Every morning I get up, my car has another key mark on it. I have gone to bed and woken up to find him standing over me. No one seems to be able to help. The police said that because he lived there, his fingerprints would be all over the house anyway and unless they have solid proof, it is a he said, she said case. I was too ashamed to tell my family all that is happening. I cannot eat, sleep, or even take care of the children properly. I can't take it anymore. I just can't take it anymore!"

The tears flowed I felt like my life had gone down the drain along with what little strength I had left.

"Michelle, it is okay, but is that the reason why you attempted to kill yourself?"

"I just want the pain to stop. I know it was wrong. How could I do this to my beautiful children? Who would have been there for them? My beautiful Santana, who would be there when it's time for her prom, or Rashaun, my sweet boy? He has special needs, you know. Who would be there to help him? How could I do this? How could I do this? I just want it all to stop."

"It will, Michelle, it will, as you did the right thing by getting in touch. I always say to my clients that no one can answer a phone call that wasn't made. You have made the call, and we are here to help you. You are stronger than you know. I read through your notes and realised that, while dealing with all of this, you recently had an operation to have a tumour removed. I assume all went well?"

I replied with a nod of the head.

"Michelle, it's not too late to turn your life around. With the right help, you will be fine. You will be there to look after your children, but in order to do that, you have to first take care of yourself. I can see from your notes here that one of your favourite hobbies is writing. Well, guess what? You have the ability to rewrite your history and turn things around. You just have to allow yourself to accept help."

Rewrite my history, turn a new leaf...what did Nicky ask me again? Oh yes, do I think it is possible to write my life away? Now, here this counsellor is, telling me that I have the ability to rewrite my history.

Have you ever had a time in your life when you wished that your life was actually a physical book where you could go back and rip out the pages of the things in the past you did not like or weren't happy about, maybe that ex or that costly mistake that you made? Unfortunately, that's not possible. But I realised at that moment that I may not be able to rip out the pages, but I could make a difference for my future. With the help of the counselor, my whilst church, friends, and family, you would have seen me stepping into my power. You would have seen me on a spiritual journey while also working on myself through personal development. I started reading self-development books like Dale Carnegie's 'How to Win Friends and Influence People,' Robin Sharma's 'The Saint, The Surfer, and The CEO,' Joyce Meyer's 'Battlefield of the Mind,' Spencer Johnson, 'Who Moved My Cheese?' and Willie Jolley's 'A Setback is a Setup For A Comeback.' I started to listen to powerful people like Les Brown, Lisa Nichols, Tony Robbins, and Jim Rohn. You would have seen me on a spiritual journey as well as attending seminars, Mastercoach, and the Coaching Academy to achieve my accreditation as a Life Coach. The Mpowerment Ltd is where I learned NLP (Neuro Linguistic Programming), and you would have seen me finding out who Michelle truly was. I then decided that I wanted to help people as well, just like how I was helped. I wanted to help others with my story, so I signed up for a programme to write my book, so I could share it and help even if it was one reader who would read it.

Now, there were some people on the way. You know those ones - the Naysayers. "So what qualifies you to write a book?" "Will anybody buy your book when they don't even know you?" "You went through depression and attempted suicide; how can you be qualified to write a book in order to help others – are you for real?" "So, you think you are JK Rowling now, huh?" However, I decided that even if the book just helped me to get everything out there, then that would be enough. So, nevertheless, I wrote the book and started to attend and speak at events where people were coming up to me, slowly but surely, and saying, "Wow, your story was amazing." "You need to share this story; it really helped and inspired me."

This was all great, but I had used up the last of my savings to write the book. And now that I did and I was inspiring others with my story, my pocket was not feeling a bit inspired (Ha,Ha). The business that I had in mind seemed terribly far away.

At this point, I had now used all my savings, wages, and sold items to invest in personal development. My now new husband Allain thought I was mad, but I told myself that when I made my money back, I could always replace them. I had now learned that I needed to get my message out to more people -- not just one-on-one, not just one person reading my book -- but that I could share the message of hope and help to as many people who, just like me, got dealt a bad card. That's why I decided to take action. Because I wanted to help those who have been on that road, just like me. But the question was how?

After much dedication and commitment my first book Overcome & Rise Above was not only published but also became a bestseller, and though this was great as it ramped up my authority, not much was happening financially. I had started my business on the side as a Certified Life Coach whilst juggling my job as a train driver, and it was moving, but slowly. I was going from one mentorship programme to the next, attending the seminars, getting psyched up, returning home, and back to square one, as I had no idea what to do or anyone to be accountable to. It became frustrating as I kept meeting other authors like myself that had a book, but then that was it. They were not known or earning anything. I kept hearing the common story of how they spent all this money to write their book or start their business, but then that was it. I started to retrace my steps to what had brought me this far, what I had put in place that worked, remembering a statement I had heard from one of my mentors. I then decided at that moment to write down all the challenges I was currently facing and see how I could solve them.

I had a powerful idea - to turn my pain into profits. The question was, how could I make it happen? The answer was clear - by selling the solution. That's when I embarked on writing my second book, "Rise Above and Believe." I poured my heart and soul into it, taking on the roles of writer, editor, and designer. Within just 90 days, I had completed the entire process and published it, all based on the formula I had discovered in my newfound solution. But I didn't stop there. I also developed the modules for my coaching program and started using my book as a business tool to attract new clients. My efforts did not go unnoticed, as I received a commendation from the Late Her Majesty the Queen. This recognition propelled me to become an advocate for parents with children with special needs and women who had experienced domestic abuse. I began leveraging media releases and securing TV and radio interviews. The demand for my speaking engagements increased, and I even started hosting my own events.

The first event I created was Women Be - a powerful platform for women's empowerment and networking. Through this experience and the knowledge I gained, I was able to build my business and establish multiple streams of income. I approached this journey with careful consideration, analysing what worked and what didn't. If I got it right, I knew this service could be packaged and sold to help others find their own success.

I am absolutely thrilled to share with you that I did achieve that significant milestone! I successfully developed a programme that specifically catered to supporting business owners and entrepreneurs in writing their own business books and leveraging them as powerful marketing tools. Through my own experience, I had discovered the immense potential of this approach, and I became dedicated to helping others unlock their full potential.

The next phase of my entrepreneurial journey revolved around guiding individuals with incredible ideas on how to transform them into profitable business ventures. By this time I also had taken on the role of being one of Andy Harrington's mentor at the Professional Speakers Academy and this undoubtedly contributed to the growth in my speaking skills.

As I dedicated myself to this path, my efforts started to gain recognition and led to a series of remarkable accomplishments. I was humbled to receive prestigious awards, including the title of Mentor of the Year and multiple speaker awards. This success opened doors for me to speak on an international scale and gain even more recognition for my work. I was also honored with notable titles, such as Performance Coach of the Year, ACE Mentor of the Year, and Empowerment Woman of the Year, among others. These accolades served as a testament to the impact I was making in the lives of others and inspired me to continue dedicating myself to mentoring and empowering individuals to achieve their goals. As I continued this fulfilling journey, I had the privilege of mentoring and guiding a diverse range of individuals, from business owners to professional boxers and singers. Furthermore, I had the pleasure of publishing numerous authors who not only achieved bestselling status but also received distinguished awards. To my great delight, even my youngest daughter, Alisha, who was just six years old at the time, became a published author and award winner at The Global Author Awards. I can confidently say that I am living out my purpose and leaving a lasting impact on this earth to ensure that future generations are aware of my presence but more importantly that I am helping others to also give birth to their vision. One of the greatest joys I experience today is providing training and assistance to others in transforming their ideas into profitable programs and products. Witnessing them not only bring their desired visions to life but also deserving the success they achieve fills my heart with tremendous joy. I take special pride in witnessing the growth and transformation of women who, like me, once doubted the possibility of achieving success.

In addition to my business success, I have recently experienced an even greater joy, of being ordained as a deacon in my church, allowing me to be actively involved in the work of God. It brings me immense fulfilment to serve and connect with the incredible women in my community, as I now co-lead the women's ministry.

Living life on my terms has always been a deep desire of mine, aligning it with God's will for me. Achieving time and financial freedom has been a crucial goal, not just for myself but also to inspire and guide others in achieving the same. I share my story not to boast (God Forbid) but with the intention of igniting a spark of inspiration within you. You possess the power to accomplish extraordinary feats and leave an enduring legacy. Start walking that together, with the right guidance and support you can make it happen. I am eagerly anticipating the remarkable achievements you will undoubtedly accomplish on your own unique path.

As I sit here in my office and the memories come flooding through, I never ever dreamt I would have been able to pull myself from that dark place that I once was, there is still so much that I still have not shared with you, as the story would never end. The truth really is that your story never ends, until you have left this earth. It does in some way continue even after death. If a legacy is left for others to follow on from and that has always been one of my greatest desires. It is important for me to emphasise that despite the progress I have made in my journey, it doesn't mean that challenges no longer arise. I have faced and continue to face numerous hurdles that I must overcome.

There is a tendency for some individuals to present a picture-perfect life, hiding the realities they face behind closed doors. They strive to maintain a professional and flawless image in the public eye, creating an illusion of smooth sailing and complete control. However, I strongly believe in authenticity and allowing others to see our vulnerabilities. This does not mean seeking sympathy, but rather being open and genuine. It is through being real that others can truly learn and be inspired. I have always maintained that I would never seek a mentor who claims to have never faced any challenges or difficulties in life. How can they guide and support me during my own hard times if they haven't experienced them personally?

In life, we all encounter difficult moments, although they may vary from person to person. Each of us has a unique story to share and lessons to impart. You may feel that your experiences are not as extreme as something like domestic abuse or attempted suicide, but that does not diminish the value or worthiness of your story. Every story has the power to inspire and connect.

Remember, authenticity and vulnerability are not weaknesses but strengths. Embrace your own journey and share your story, for it is through these shared experiences that we can uplift and support one another.

On this journey, I have learned valuable lessons that I would like to share with you:

> *Success does not define you,*
> *but you define success.*
> **HAZEL BREEN**

You have the power to determine your own success. Your worth as an individual is not merely measured by external achievements, but also by who you are and who you become. It is essential to resist the urge to let others define what success means for you, as no one truly knows your strengths. In fact, you may not even realise your own strengths until you face challenges that test them. Creating your own definition of success should guide your life choices. Success is subjective and trying to gauge it based on someone else>s standards will hinder your progress. If you are not where you want to be yet, remember that it is still possible to achieve your goals. Keep them in sight, believe in yourself, and refuse to settle for less than you deserve.

> *You don't have to be great to start, but*
> *you have to start to achieve greatness.*
> **ZIG ZIGLAR**

No one starts off as a great person. Every extraordinary individual had to persevere through difficult times on their journey. We all begin at the starting point, so stop telling yourself that you are not good enough or knowledgeable enough. Take one step at a time and gather the necessary resources as you go along. Comparing yourself to others may discourage you, so focus on running your own race. Remember that it's not about how quickly you finish, but about enduring until the end.

> *You might not be able to erase the pages of your past that you're unhappy with, but you have the power to determine what will be written in the next chapter of your book called life.*
> MICHELLE WATSON

Life is a journey with a destined purpose, and along the way, we face numerous challenges that prepare us for our ultimate destination. Take a moment to reflect on the people you are currently or aspire to help in the future. You will likely realise that your own experiences have guided you to this path. While I cannot change what happened to me, I made the conscious decision not to let it dictate my future or legacy. I refuse to be remembered as a victim of domestic abuse; instead, I aim to be seen as a survivor and a voice of influence. Living your life based on others' expectations makes you a mere shell of a person. I urge you to remember this crucial point:

> *The moment you sacrifice your own life for others' approval is the moment you stop truly living.*
> MICHELLE WATSON

I had reached a point where I stopped truly living and the only way I could change that was by letting go of the past and embracing the future I desired. The choice is yours: continue to be governed by what you've been through and dwell in the pages of the past or open a new chapter in your book of life. It is time to start believing in and living for yourself. Be authentic, not just the version of yourself that you want others to see, but the version that feels joy, satisfaction, fulfilment, and happiness in what you do.

Now is the time to share yourself with the world. You have overcome dark moments, and it is your duty to be a light for those who may stumble along the way. If they fall, let them see your light so they can rise and keep walking. Keep pushing forward, believe in yourself, and remember that your story has the power to inspire and uplift others.

> *A story not shared is a message not heard and a life not saved.*
> MICHELLE WATSON

- *Are you stuck in the Past?*
- *Live in the Present*
- *Progress – It's time for growth*
- *Purpose – Plan – Proceed*
- *The permanent pause*

Personal Development is Necessary

CHAPTER TWO

Personal Development is Necessary

"Your past does not define your present, and your present does not dictate your future. Embrace the lessons learned, live fully in the present, and fearlessly create the future you envision."

MICHELLE WATSON

Now that we've laid the groundwork and you know more about my journey and what motivates me, it's time to shift the focus back onto YOU and your incredible journey towards becoming the dynamic Eikonic woman you were born to be. As I walked this path, I discovered something vital that propelled me forward and sustained me through it all: personal growth. It became my anchor, alongside my faith in God and the support of my community. Girl, let me tell you, I had to put in the work on myself, and that's where Personal Development truly made a difference.

One common mistake I often observe among entrepreneurs is overlooking the importance of personal growth while pouring all their energy into building their business and others. But here's the thing: you may be working on bringing your vision to life, but it's equally crucial to invest in developing yourself as the visionary, the person who will bring that vision to fruition. There's a saying that resonates deeply with me: "Your talent can open doors, but it's your character that will keep you there."

Recognising the significance of personal development and committing to your own growth will create a solid foundation for your journey as an empowered Eikonic woman. It's about honing your skills, expanding your knowledge, and nurturing your mindset. Embracing personal development allows you to bring out your best self, equipped to face any challenge that comes your way. Remember, personal growth isn't a one-time event or a destination you arrive at. It's a continuous, lifelong process of self-improvement and self-discovery. As you invest in your personal development, you'll uncover hidden strengths, unveil new passions, and cultivate a mindset that sets you up for success. It's an ongoing journey of transformation and growth that enables you to reach your fullest potential. The journey of becoming your most extraordinary self is a remarkable journey, so let's navigate the path of personal development a little bit and look at a few relevant phases I had to address, enabling me to achieve remarkable growth. I will encourage you to in your own potential, embrace personal development, and watch as your character blooms and sustains you on the path to greatness.

> *Your talent can open doors, but it's your character that will keep you there.*

Remember, I'm always here to support and encourage you as you embark on this journey. Feel free to reach out whenever you need guidance or simply want to share your progress. You are a beacon of inspiration, and I can't wait to witness the incredible woman you are becoming.

YOUR PAST

Have you addressed your PAST?

You may be wondering, "Well Michelle, you said that I should let go of my past! Why are you confusing me?" A common misconception that most clients, I have had the privilege of working with, have had is that they believe letting go of their past is about burying it. Now, what do I mean by burying? I mean brushing it off or pushing it to the back of the mind and moving on by trying to convince themselves that they have let it go, until it resurfaces at some point when that part of the past gets triggered by a present situation. To let go means that you actually address it, deal with it upfront so that it no longer raises issues later on or becomes one of the common words of today - Trigger.

Letting go of your past is a powerful act of self-love and growth. It means releasing the shackles that have kept you anchored to old wounds, regrets, and pain. It's about embracing the beautiful truth that you deserve to move forward with grace and freedom. When you let go of your past, you FREE yourself from the heavy burden that has weighed you down for far too long. You allow yourself to BREAKFREE not bury yourself under the weights of resentment, guilt, and self-blame. It doesn't mean forgetting or denying what happened; instead, it's about facing it full on and choosing to rise above it and reclaim your power. It's creating a space for healing and transformation, giving yourself the chance to heal old wounds and nurture your emotional well-being. This is a courageous act of self-compassion, allowing yourself to heal from the pain and disappointment that may have held you captive.

It is very important to remember that your past holds great significance and also contributes to shaping your present and future.

For example, when you look back at my own story, you will see moments where seeds got planted in my life. To move forward, I had to uproot and discard those seeds along the way.

For instance, fear was deeply ingrained in me, stemming not only from the fear of falling in love again but also the fear of failure. I no longer trusted my decision making. After all, I made the decision to have an abuser as a husband and father to my child. Negative experiences had led me to believe that I would never be good enough, fueling my fear of acceptance.

The next one was unforgiveness... let's talk about it – let's go there!

It's not always easy to forgive, is it? We hear advice telling us to forgive, but the reality is far more complex. Please don't feel guilty if your initial response was 'NO'. Believe me, I truly understand that feeling. In fact, it takes tremendous strength to forgive, contrary to what some may believe. Looking back, I recall how difficult it was for me to forgive. After everything I went through and the mistakes I made, I found myself hating not only my ex-husband but also myself. I blamed myself for the wrong choices and the impact they had on my life and my children's lives. It took immense strength to forgive not just my ex, but also myself. Being unable to do so kept me stagnant for far too long.

Perhaps you've questioned whether it's possible to hate yourself or even forgive yourself. Unfortunately, there are many people unknowingly carrying resentment towards themselves, and forgiving oneself can be even more challenging than forgiving others. I carried a deep hatred for my ex-husband to the point where the mere mention of his name would make my blood boil. I would attend events and hastily leave as soon as he entered, not realising how it was only damaging my own life and robbing me of true freedom.

Have you ever found yourself consumed by bitterness towards someone who has wronged you, while they effortlessly continue with their own life?

It's a heavy burden to carry, isn't it?

But what I came to realise is that real forgiveness is about finding inner peace. It's about letting go of the anger and resentment that weighs you down, because that is the only way to truly free yourself. When you release those negative emotions, the real you can shine brightly. But here's the thing about forgiveness: it's not a one-time event. It's an ongoing process. You may think you have forgiven someone, until they show up or a similar situation arises, and suddenly those negative emotions come welling up again. It can be frustrating, and it can feel like you're taking steps backwards. But sis, please know that you are not alone in this struggle. I have been there too, and I understand that it takes time and effort to truly forgive. I believed that I had forgiven my ex, and outwardly I would engage in conversations and display all the right gestures when I encountered him. However, there came a moment of profound realisation when I discovered that traces of bitterness still lingered within me.

It's a bit like rinsing a glass with water, thinking it is clean, only to discover lurking residue at the bottom. This analogy mirrored my internal struggle, as my true feelings sharply contrasted with the facade I presented to the world. Despite my efforts to deceive others, and even myself, it was I who was consumed by the truth.

But then, a wave of joy washed over me when I reaches a point where I no longer felt any emotional reaction when communicating with or encountering him, even amidst ridicule and verbal abuse over the phone. Instead, I responded calmly with expressions of gratitude or blessings. And then, the day arrived when he reached out to me, expressing genuine remorse and seeking forgiveness. In that profound moment, I was able to sincerely reply, "You are already forgiven." I could now think of him, hear his voice, and see his face without harboring any negative thoughts. It was the embodiment of true forgiveness.

The veil of gratitude descended upon me, as I embraced the journey my experience with him had set me on. I chose to see him not as an enemy, but as an unknowing protagonist in my story. Drawing from the wisdom found in Genesis 50:20-22, where Joseph forgave his brothers who had sold him into slavery, I found solace in the belief that God can use even evil actions for good. Just as Joseph and Jesus faced adversity that ultimately shaped their purpose and destiny, I recognised that my ex's actions, though intended for evil, had propelled me towards my own path.

It may seem foolish to some, but I draw inspiration from 1 Corinthians 1:20-31, which reminds us that what may be foolishness to man can be wisdom to God. By choosing forgiveness and taking the direction guided by God, I have witnessed countless people being encouraged and blessed. If I had remained bitter and held onto unforgiveness, I firmly believe that the trajectory of my life would not have shifted in such a transformative way.

Letting go of the bitterness and resentment that once dwelled within me has been a liberating experience. I have learned that forgiveness is not just a mere declaration, or a show put on for others; it is a transformative process that takes place within the depths of our being. It sets us free from the chains of past pain and enables us to embrace a future untainted by grudges. I share this to remind you that forgiveness is a journey, often filled with layers to be unravelled. It requires self-awareness, honesty, and a willingness to confront the lingering echoes of hurt. Embrace the joy that awaits when you can genuinely let go and release the negativity. Remember, true forgiveness is not a weakness but a strength that empowers us to reclaim our own peace and happiness. You are not doing it for the benefit of the other person or letting them off scotch-free but instead, you are doing it for your benefit; you are the one that will be free.

Indeed, forgiveness is a remarkable act of healing, a cleansing of the soul, a precious gift of liberation and authentic empowerment. The essence of true forgiveness lies in fostering compassion towards those who have wronged us and releasing the burdens that hold us captive. It is a delightful sensation to soar through life like a bird, untethered and unencumbered, with no lingering animosity towards anyone, including ourselves. I want you to take this which I am about to say to you in, write it down, put it somewhere visible where you can see it daily. Choosing to forgive is not you doing a favour to the individual that has hurt you but instead you are doing yourself a favour! We may think that by holding onto these negative emotions, we are somehow punishing the person who hurt us. However, in reality, we are only inflicting further pain upon ourselves.

Forgiving does not mean forgetting or condoning the hurtful actions of others. It does not mean that we have to maintain a relationship with the person who harmed us or that we have to trust them again. Forgiveness is a personal journey that focuses on our own well-being and growth. By forgiving, we reclaim our power and regain control over our emotions. We no longer allow the actions of others to define us or dictate our happiness. Instead, we choose to take charge of our own lives and break free from the negative cycle that keeps us trapped in pain.

In the end, choosing to forgive is about prioritising our own emotional well-being and refusing to let the actions of others control our happiness. By embracing forgiveness, we allow ourselves to live a more fulfilling and joyful life.

> *Choosing to forgive is not you doing a favour to the individual that has hurt you but instead you are doing yourself a favour!*

The impact of our past experiences can manifest in various ways, affecting our self-esteem, breeding doubt, and eroding trust. For you, it may not be unforgiveness, but there is always something lurking from the past, creating those limiting beliefs that expose its head at some vital decision-making moments in your life. For example, low self-esteem may stem from enduring ridicule and fostering apprehension over others' opinions, leading to a lack of belief in our own capabilities. Having lived with someone who exhibited split personalities forced me to tread cautiously, unsure of what to expect next, which bred deep-seated doubt. To shield myself from potential disappointment, I found it easier to embrace doubt rather than embrace hope.

Every betrayal and hurtful experience corroded my ability to trust not only others but, more devastatingly, myself. As I mentioned earlier, if I could have made such a grave misjudgment of character and entered a relationship, even a marriage, and had children with a Jekyll and Hyde personality, I lost faith in my own decision-making capacity and judgments.

These experiences collectively shape our perception of ourselves and impact how we navigate life's complexities. However, the journey towards healing and self-restoration is possible. By acknowledging the wounds from the past, seeking support, and actively engaging in the process of forgiveness and self-discovery, we can reclaim our sense of self-worth, ignite trust in ourselves, and embrace a future brimming with possibility and fulfilment. There are many examples I am sure you could look back at, as there's so much from your past that could be holding you back, possibly even more than you realise. It could be influencing the decisions you make, like being in a car but not being the one driving. Maybe your past is the driver, while you sit comfortably in the passenger seat.

It's important to recognise that the negative experiences from your past have the potential to impact your future success. When we carry the weight of past traumas, regrets, or limiting beliefs, they act as stumbling blocks on our path to greatness. They shape our mindset and how we see ourselves. They create self-doubt and fear of repeating past mistakes. They hold us back from taking risks and stepping outside of our comfort zones. They chip away at our confidence, preventing us from fully embracing our unique gifts and talents.

Have you ever wondered why you possibly have not yet taken the step to really start living your true purpose, create your business or even scale it to the next level, despite knowing you are more than capable of doing so?

The reason why despite knowing your purpose you refuse to walk in it?

The reason why you don't trust anyone?

Why you hate men?

Why you are so fearful of taking risks?

Scared to be committed in a relationship?

Why you are constantly filled with anger?

Why you battle with unforgiveness?

Why you battle with limiting beliefs?

Why you battle with anxiety?

Why you have so much negative internal chatter?

Why you have low self-esteem or doubt your capabilities?

Stop and take a moment to think about continuing in life or being in business, carrying all these sacks. It is heavy, right?

Potentially, you are just going through the motions, keeping yourself busy because you don't want to have to address or resolve them. The problem with this is that subconsciously, you are being steered and possibly suppressed from living at your fullest potential.

Yes, our past does not define our future, but it certainly helps shape it, whether consciously or subconsciously. The experiences and events that have occurred in your life contributes to your growth, knowledge, and resilience. They have shaped our perspectives, values, and beliefs, all of which play a crucial role in determining our path forward. The mistakes we've made in the past have taught us valuable lessons, providing insight into what works and what doesn't. The successes we've achieved have fuelled our confidence and motivation, showing us what is possible. Furthermore, the relationships we've formed, the skills we've acquired, and the challenges we've overcome have all contributed to our personal and professional development. While again, the past does not dictate our future, it does serve as a foundation upon which one can build. By harnessing the lessons from your past, setting goals, and taking deliberate action, you have the power to shape a future that aligns with your aspirations and fulfils your potential.

Embrace the experiences of your past, learn from them, and let them propel you towards a successful and fulfilling future.

The main area that your past affects and why resolving your past is relevant is your belief system.

A belief system is a set of mutually supported beliefs. It includes beliefs that are passed down from parents, various communities, and your experiences.

Some of these beliefs, by the way, are not really "yours."

Hmmm, think about that for a minute...

If they were passed down to you without you creating them, are they really yours or were they handed to you and at some point, you then accepted them and took ownership. Many beliefs that you are holding onto about yourself as truth are most possibly false. It is important to question and challenge these beliefs in order to expand beyond limiting beliefs. It's a bit like the belief in Father Christmas. When you were a child, you most likely, just as I did, believed that Father Christmas was real (spoiler alert – lol). Now that you know the truth about Father Christmas not being real, it makes you wonder how many other beliefs you might still hold that are not true. Who told you that Father Christmas was real when you were younger? Most likely, it was your parents, who were probably told the same by their parents. It may seem very trivial, but it should make you stop and think about all the other things you have picked up on your journey and given them ownership in your life. This raises the question of how many other false beliefs have been passed down through generations. Perhaps for you, it's the belief that you're not good enough or that your dream is not possible. However, in order to accomplish things you once thought were impossible, you need to relinquish ownership of some of these beliefs and start believing in yourself.

Limiting beliefs can have negative effects on our lives, such as fear, low self-esteem, doubt, lack of trust, and working hard instead of working smart. It is crucial to identify and address these limiting beliefs in order to move forward and create a better future.

Your past experiences and beliefs shape your blueprint, which is like a guide for creating your world and living your life. It is important to be aware of and admit the limiting beliefs that you carry from your past. You also need to understand how these beliefs developed and affirm new positive beliefs to replace them. Letting go of the past is essential for living in the present and creating the future you desire.

By changing your beliefs and using your past experiences to grow and help others, you can overcome challenges and fulfill your purpose in life. It is time to let go of the past and experience inner peace.

Let's imagine a massive, beautiful ship full of potential. Everyone is ready to set sail and embark on a journey. But if that ship remains anchored, it won't be able to go anywhere but only rock to and fro with the waves of the sea, no matter how much potential it holds. Your life is similar to that ship. You may have degrees, qualifications, and immense potential, but imagine all the chains from your past attached to you like an anchor. These include limiting beliefs, traumatic experiences, and negative words that have been spoken to you. These chains are holding you back and preventing you from reaching your full potential. So, I ask you, how far will you go with these chains weighing you down? You will stay at the edge, rocking to and fro but going nowhere. It's important to acknowledge that your past is relevant and has a hand in shaping you. However, contrary to popular belief, your past does not always have to be negative. In fact, it is through the challenging experiences and pain that your passion can emerge. It all depends on how you choose to handle these situations – that is what leaves the lasting factor.

In life, it's not the challenges themselves that matter the most, instead, it's how you deal with those challenges. Your decisions and actions today will shape your future. It's up to you to determine the outcome and create the future you desire. You need to take steps in changing your life blueprint.

A blueprint serves as a guide or plan for creating something. Typically, it is used in the construction industry to direct the building process of a house or building.

Now, let's apply this concept to your own life. Your blueprint consists of the beliefs, patterns, and moral guidelines that shape how you create your world and live your life. It's important to acknowledge that at one point, my past made me feel like a failure. However, I realised that I had the power to change this perception. As Les Brown wisely states, "Someone's opinion of you is not who you are." Interestingly, even your own opinion of yourself may not accurately reflect who you truly are. My past kept me confined in a dark room, but in order to create the life I desired, I needed to break free from that darkness.

> ## *Someone's opinion of you is not who you are.*
> **LES BROWN**

So, how can you prevent your past from negatively impacting your present and future? It's essential to address your beliefs, remove any obstacles or blockages, and actively declare new positive and limitless beliefs. By doing so, you can overcome the limitations imposed by your past and create a brighter future.

Start the journey by applying the five A's below:

- **Ask**: Your first step may be to ask for help. For me I prayed, asking God for help and guidance to be able to do the next 4 A's to also connect me with the people I will need to help me i.e counsellor, therapist, pastor, mentor etc. not everyone is the right person to help you but help is necessary. I don't believe it is a journey you should venture on your own so please ASK FOR HELP!

- **Awareness**: You need to be aware of the experiences that happened in your life from childhood which have affected you the most. You need to know what is wrong before you can fix it.

- **Admit**: As well as becoming aware, you need to also admit you are carrying that limiting belief and accept how it is affecting you. There is no way you can change a limiting belief before admitting you have it.

- **Account**: Have an account of how you developed or learned that belief, figure out at what point did this chain start holding you back, and this could be very significant to how you need to get rid of it.

- **Affirm**: This is normally the most difficult step but one of the most important. This is to prove the opposite of the limiting belief you have and affirm the belief you want. All the seeds I spoke about earlier can be fixed by changing that belief to what you really want it to be – your own belief. You can either allow your past to make you or break you, and I was allowing my past to break me. I was using it as an excuse to give up rather than looking at it as a challenge that I would eventually be able to overcome and rise above. When I finally got the understanding of it, I was then able to turn the downside of those challenges into the upside of renewing my life, and I decided to use my past and experiences to help others and become a big part of my WHY – my purpose.

I once read in an article that one's ability to envision the future is strongly influenced by memories, as you tend to use memories of past experiences to predict what your life will be like in the future. Hence, you come across some people who will say their life is not going to amount to anything in the future because all they have had in the past is bad luck. You have the power within you to address these wounds, to heal, and to break free from the limitations imposed by your past. It won't be easy, but by facing them, seeking support, therapy, and engaging in the journey of forgiveness and healing, you can lighten your load and live a more fulfilled life.

Letting go of your past means embracing the wisdom and lessons it has taught you. It's about recognising that your experiences, both good and bad, have shaped you into the remarkable woman you are today. By acknowledging the lessons and growth that came from your past, you pave the way for a brighter future. As you let go of your past, be gentle with yourself. Healing is not linear, and it's okay to have moments of struggle or setbacks. Celebrate the progress you make, no matter how small, and trust that you have the strength within you to create a future filled with joy, growth, and limitless possibilities. I am honoured to be a part of your journey, supporting you as you let go of your past and step into a future brimming with endless potential. Embrace this beautiful process of healing and growth. The road ahead may not always be easy, but I wholeheartedly believe that it's worth it. You are capable of extraordinary things, and I can't wait to witness your transformation unfold.

No Time Like the Present

So where are you right now?

Maybe you find yourself reflecting on past situations that have kept you feeling stuck. These experiences might have left you with a lingering sense of disappointment, clouding your perspective and hindering your progress. When you constantly dwell on these setbacks, it can be challenging to move forward and embrace new opportunities. Recognising the consequences of allowing this cloud of disappointment to hover over you is crucial for your growth and happiness. By fixating on the past and feeling stuck, you may miss out on the present moment and the potential it holds. It's essential to acknowledge the past but putting a process in place to help you, rather than dwelling on negative experiences, will prevent you from perpetuating feelings of frustration and aid in making meaningful changes. Instead of dwelling in the past, what you should be doing is shifting your focus towards the lessons learned from those past situations. Use them as steppingstones for personal growth and self-improvement.

Recognising the impact of past experiences is the first step towards freeing yourself from that cloud of disappointment. Embrace forgiveness for yourself and others involved and let go of any lingering resentment. Realise that staying trapped in the past hinders your ability to fully appreciate the present and create a positive future. Being aware of the patterns that have kept you feeling stuck and consciously choosing to break free from them, you open yourself up to new possibilities and a brighter outlook. Focus on your strengths, desires, and aspirations, and take intentional steps towards your goals. Embrace the opportunities that come your way and have faith in your ability to navigate through challenges.

Remember, you have the power to shape your own narrative and determine your path forward. Release yourself from the weight of disappointment, embrace the present moment, and confidently move towards a future filled with growth, fulfilment, and happiness.

It's possible that you are in a state of movement, but not at the pace you desire. This can lead to frustration and anxiety, causing you to feel stressed and overwhelmed. The sense of discontentment and impatience can cause you to lose sight of the progress you have made and the potential that lies ahead. It's essential to recognise that success and growth take time and patience. By being kinder to yourself and acknowledging the progress you have made, you can alleviate the anxiety and frustration that come with the feeling of being "stuck" in life. Accepting that growth is a gradual process can help you shift your focus towards the opportunities available in the present moment, leading to a more positive and fulfilling life experience. Perhaps you have been settling for second best all your life, either because you think you don't deserve it or have the ability to achieve it. Staying in positions, jobs, relationships, and a mindset that does not value your worth, potential, or level you up to the best you could be. Here's the thing, having a clear understanding of where you are now is a powerful practice that can bring clarity and insight into your life. By acknowledging your current circumstances, both externally and internally, you gain a deeper understanding of your present reality. This self-awareness allows you to assess your strengths, weaknesses, desires, and challenges. It helps you make informed decisions and take purposeful actions in alignment with your values and goals. Realising where you are now also enables you to appreciate and accept your current situation, whether it's a moment of success, a period of transition, or a challenging time. It encourages gratitude for what you have and cultivates resilience in the face of uncertainty. By embracing your present location on your life's journey, you can navigate with intention and create a meaningful path forward.

Living in the present moment allows you to fully acknowledge and appreciate your current abilities and the opportunities that are right in front of you. When you are fully present, you can better understand your strengths, talents, and skills. This self-awareness enables you to make the most of your current circumstances and seize the opportunities that align with your abilities. Moreover, being present allows you to cultivate a sense of gratitude for what you have and the opportunities that present themselves in your life. When you are fully engaged in the present moment, you can recognise the blessings and possibilities that surround you. This positive mindset opens the door for new experiences and growth. By staying present, you can also overcome any obstacles or challenges that may arise. When you are fully aware of the current situation, you can respond with clarity, creativity, and resourcefulness. Rather than getting caught up in worries about the future or dwelling on past mistakes, you can focus on the present moment and take decisive action. By fully embracing the present, you can create a fulfilling and purposeful life that aligns with your true potential. So, take a moment to pause, breathe, and appreciate the opportunities that are right in front of you. I believe this is something that many women miss. They spend so much time being stressed about the past and anxious about the future that they are unable to be grateful for what they have and where they are currently. If you are in a place of grumbling, all you will be paying attention to is the issue and not the solution. It is the solution that will bring about change, yet it is surprising that so many individuals dwell in the 'I have a problem mode,' which does not serve or bring about a difference. With everything in life there is a time and a season Ecclesiates 3 tells us this. There is a time to sow and a time to reap, if you remain in the sowing season you will indeed miss the harvest? Or if you remain in the reaping season what do you think is going to happen, there will soon be nothing to reap because you did not re-enter the sowing period. You just need to pay attention to and understand the time you are in. I once preached a sermon during a preaching series at my church around Kairos & Chronos. The sermon was titled 'Force Ripe' I spoke about people not living in the present moment, where they were either stuck in the past or so anxious about their future that they become overly busy trying to forcefully create it.

Force Ripe
Sermon

https://qrco.de/bf1xZ4

Living in the present moment has numerous benefits that go beyond recognising your abilities and seizing opportunities. When you are fully present, you experience a deeper sense of contentment and fulfilment in your daily life, and that is a great starting point.

One of the advantages of living in the present is enhanced self-awareness. By anchoring yourself in the present moment, you become more attuned to your thoughts, emotions, and physical sensations. This heightened self-awareness allows you to better understand yourself, your values, and your aspirations. It enables you to make conscious choices and align your actions with your authentic self. Acknowledging and staying in the present moment also cultivates a greater sense of mindfulness. Mindfulness entails being fully engaged and attentive to the present moment, without judgment. When you practice mindfulness, you develop a heightened ability to appreciate the small moments of joy, beauty, and connection that often go unnoticed when your mind is preoccupied with the past or future. Furthermore, it fosters stronger relationships and connections with others. When you are fully focused and present during interactions, you develop better listening skills and demonstrate genuine interest. This not only strengthens connections but also enriches the quality of your relationships.

You will be able to alleviate unnecessary stress and anxiety. Many worries and anxieties stem from dwelling on the past or fretting about the future. By redirecting your attention to the present moment, you free yourself from the burden of past regrets or future uncertainties. This allows you to fully embrace life as it unfolds, reducing stress and creating a greater sense of ease and balance.

In summary, living in the present moment not only helps you recognise your abilities and seize opportunities but also enhances self-awareness, cultivates mindfulness, strengthens relationships, and reduces stress, enabling you to not work from a place of anxiety. By choosing to be fully present in each moment, you can create a more meaningful, fulfilling, and joyful life.

One of the advantages of living in the present is enhanced self-awareness. By anchoring yourself in the present moment, you become more attuned to your thoughts, emotions, and physical sensations. This heightened self-awareness allows you to better understand yourself, your values, and your aspirations. It enables you to make conscious choices and align your actions with your authentic self. Acknowledging and staying in the present moment also cultivates a greater sense of mindfulness. Mindfulness entails being fully engaged and attentive to the present moment, without judgment. When you practice mindfulness, you develop a heightened ability to appreciate the small moments of joy, beauty, and connection that often goes unnoticed when your mind is preoccupied with the past or future. Furthermore, it fosters stronger relationships and connections with others. When you are fully focused and present during interactions, you develop better listening skills and demonstrate genuine interest. This not only strengthens connections but also enriches the quality of your relationships.

You will be able to alleviate unnecessary stress and anxiety. Many worries and anxieties stem from dwelling on the past or fretting about the future. By redirecting your attention to the present moment, you free yourself from the burden of past regrets or future uncertainties. This allows you to fully embrace life as it unfolds, reducing stress and creating a greater sense of ease and balance.

Living in the present moment is a concept that has been discussed and promoted by many spiritual teachers, psychologists, and self-help gurus. However, despite the numerous benefits that come with being present, us women, in particular, often struggle with living in the present. There can be various reasons why women find it hard to be present and fully engaged in the moment. Here are some factors that I myself had struggled with:

1. **The pressure to multitask**: We are often expected to juggle multiple responsibilities, both at home and at work. This can create a constant pressure to do more and multitask even more, leaving little time for being fully present in the moment. I was constantly in an element of being busy and focusing on one need which was to accomplish everything on the to-do list. If not careful, this can leave you feeling like you can't afford to take a break or slow down, which inhibits the ability to focus on the present and also leads to burnout.

2. **Perfectionism**: Ladies you know that this is so high up on your list (LOL) the constant need to be a perfectionists, which can lead to a focus on the flaws and faults in yourselves. This preoccupation with perfection tends to lead to chronic self-doubt, anxiety, and fear of mistakes. Focusing too much on the past or future to avoid mistakes or assess past experiences can lead to a lack of presence and rob one of the joys of the present moment. We will be speaking a bit more about this shortly.

3. **Comparisons and self-doubt**: Oh boy, the comparison syndrome - ready to compare yourself with everyone on social media, judging yourself by arbitrary standards of beauty, success, or wealth. This comparison can lead to feelings of inadequacy that can rob one of the joys of what they have or capabilities in this present moment. Comparing oneself to others can lead to a focus on what one lacks, instead of what one already possesses, which can lead to dissatisfaction

and a lack of presence. Before you know it, you are lashing out on God in prayer – 'but God, I'm serving you, I am going to church Sunday after Sunday and fasting but yet X that went to school with me is driving, has a business and I am still at the starting blocks.' – Oops did I hit a nerve?

4. **Overthinking**: I used to tend to overthink situations and problems instead of focusing on the present moment. This led to an analysis-paralysis state that prevented me from taking action or enjoying experiences in the present. Overthinking can also lead to excessive worry and stress, which, as you know, is far from a good combination. This caused me to miss so much opportunities and kept myself in a place of regret – the 'shoulda, coulda, never' dilemma.

5. **Trauma or past experiences**: Traumatic experiences from the past can cause difficulty focusing, as triggers often arise from certain situations or events. Negative past experiences can limit one's ability to be fully present because they can cause feelings of stress or fear that interfere with the ability to experience joy and beauty around oneself, and prevent the taking of action.

6. **Lack of self-care or prioritising**: This one right here was my biggest battle, always prioritising the needs of others over my own, making it difficult to find time for self-care practices that promote mindfulness and being present. Not making time for oneself can lead to an imbalance of physical, emotional, and spiritual well-being, which can affect the ability to live in the present moment.

7. **Technology and social media**: As women spend a considerable amount of time on social media and with technology, it can be distracting and prevent us from being

present in our own lives and with those around us. From struggling to be present at work due to constantly checking our phones to feeling overwhelmed with notifications and messages, it can be challenging to disconnect from technology and practice mindfulness, and be fully present in the moment. Take a moment to think about your screen time, check how much of it was for your spiritual life, business, growth or well-being versus watching what others are doing.

> *By choosing to be fully present in each moment, you can create a more meaningful, fulfilling, and joyful life.*

Therefore, learning to live in the present moment can be a challenge for women for many reasons. By identifying the factors that are preventing you from being present, you can take steps towards overcoming these obstacles and experiencing the joy and beauty of every moment. Recognising the limitations preventing you from being present is the first step to counteract these obstacles and practice mindfulness. Making time for oneself, setting boundaries, small daily grounding exercises, and participating in a healthy ecosystem of positive relationships and activities can promote the ability to live in the present moment. It's not too late to start, and every step towards presence brings one closer to aligning with fulfilment.

Here are some strategies that can help you live in the present moment and understand the difference it can make:

1. **Cultivate mindfulness**: Mindfulness is the practice of bringing one's attention to the present moment without judgment. This practice can be integrated into daily life by engaging in activities with full awareness. By paying attention to the sights, sounds, and sensations in the present moment, you can become more anchored in the here and now. Mindfulness meditation and breathing exercises are also effective techniques to cultivate mindfulness and presence. I love to combine this with meditating on the word (a verse from the bible)

2. **Embrace self-compassion**: As women, we often hold ourselves to high standards and can be overly critical of ourselves. Practicing self-compassion involves treating oneself with kindness, understanding, and acceptance. Being present in the moment allows you to cultivate self-compassion by acknowledging your own needs, celebrating your strengths, and showing yourself the same empathy you would extend to others. This self-compassion helps you let go of self-doubt and be more present and engaged in your own growth and progress.

3. **Let go of perfectionism**: The constant pursuit of perfection can be a major obstacle to living in the present moment. You may often feel the pressure to measure up to unrealistic standards, leading to constant self-criticism and comparison. By shifting the focus from perfection to progress, you can give yourself permission to make mistakes, learn from them, and grow. Embracing imperfection allows you to be fully present in the process of growth, rather than obsessing over the end result.

4. **Practice self-care**: Taking care of yourself is essential for living in the present moment. It is important to prioritise self-care practices that nourish physical, emotional, and spiritual well-being. This can include engaging in activities that bring joy and relaxation, setting boundaries to ensure personal time and space, and nurturing yourself with healthy habits and a balanced lifestyle. When we make self-care a priority, we are better able to be present, grounded, and focused on our progress.

5. **Develop supportive relationships**: Surrounding yourself with positive and supportive relationships plays a significant role in living in the present moment. Building connections with like-minded individuals who value presence and growth creates an environment that encourages and reinforces the practice of being present. Engaging in meaningful conversations, creating space for emotional support, and being present with loved ones helps to cultivate a sense of connection and fulfilment. However, I want to emphasise that you need people around you who won't just tell you what you want to hear – the 'pleaser friend' is dangerous, but unfortunately, at times, that's the friend women gravitate to. You need a friend who will tell you the gruesome truth and hold you accountable, a friend who will push you to make the right moves – keep them very close and do not despise their open honesty or their 'not beating around the bush' attitude. Trust me, appreciate it.

Effectively applying the steps above will help you approach difficulties with resilience and help you in the areas of adaptability and problem-solving skills so that you can move forward confidently whilst embracing the present moment.

In conclusion, living in the present moment is a transformative practice for us as women. By cultivating mindfulness, embracing self-compassion, letting go of perfectionism, practicing self-care, and developing supportive relationships, you will create the experience of immense benefits of being present. This practice not only enhances personal growth but also empowers you to make progress towards your goals, leading to a more fulfilling, purpose-driven and balanced life.

Did someone say Progress?

Progress and growth to the next level in life are integral aspects of personal development and fulfilment. It involves continuous learning, improvement, and the pursuit of one's potential. Progress and growth manifest in various areas, such as personal, professional, emotional, and spiritual dimensions. Progress and growing to the next level in life involves continuous learning, adaptation, setting and pursuing goals, self-awareness, resilience, expanding comfort zones, and cultivating meaningful connections. By actively engaging in these elements, individuals can move toward their full potential, experience personal fulfilment, and continue to evolve in various dimensions of life. Embracing progress and growth is a transformative journey that allows you to reach new heights, contribute to your communities, and lead purpose-driven lives.

As we continue let us take a quick look at some defining elements of progress and growing to the next level in life:

1. **Continual learning and development**: Progress and growth require a mindset of lifelong learning. It entails actively seeking knowledge, acquiring new skills, and expanding

our understanding of ourselves and the world. This process can involve formal education, self-study, mentorship, or experiential learning. By continually developing and deepening one's knowledge and abilities, individuals can move forward and evolve in their lives.

2. **Embracing change and adaptation**: Progress and growth often involve stepping out of your comfort zone and embracing change. It requires the willingness to let go of old ways of thinking, behaving, and perceiving. Being open to new experiences, challenges, and ideas allows us to adapt and evolve. Embracing change also involves viewing obstacles and setbacks as opportunities for growth and learning, rather than as roadblocks.

3. **Setting and pursuing goals**: Progress and growth can be facilitated by setting meaningful goals and working towards your achievements. Setting specific, measurable, achievable, relevant, and time-bound (SMART) goals provides direction and focus. Additionally, breaking down larger goals into smaller, actionable steps helps to make progress more tangible and attainable. Regularly reviewing and adjusting goals allows for flexibility and continued growth.

4. **Cultivating self-awareness**: Progress and growth necessitate self-reflection and self-awareness. Understanding one's strengths, weaknesses, values, and aspirations enables individuals to make intentional choices aligned with their personal growth. Self-awareness involves recognising patterns, limiting beliefs, and areas for improvement. By developing self-awareness, you can make conscious decisions to overcome barriers and cultivate personal growth in areas that matter to you.

5. **Embracing resilience and perseverance**: Progress and growth often involve facing challenges, setbacks, and failures. Resilience and perseverance are essential qualities that will enable you to bounce back from adversities and persevere despite obstacles. A growth mindset, which focuses on continuous learning and improvement, helps individuals reframe setbacks as stepping stones towards progress. Embracing resilience and perseverance will enable you to remain committed to your growth even in the face of difficulties.

6. **Expanding our comfort zone**: Progress and growth require stepping outside of our comfort zone. It involves taking calculated risks and embracing new opportunities, even if they feel unfamiliar or challenging. By intentionally pushing boundaries and experiencing discomfort, individuals can expand their skills, knowledge, and capacity for growth. Stepping out of the comfort zone encourages personal and professional growth and enables individuals to reach the next level in their lives.

7. **Cultivating meaningful connections and support systems**: Progress and growth can be facilitated by cultivating relationships that support personal development. Meaningful connections with mentors, peers, or community members provide inspiration, guidance, and accountability. Surrounding ourselves with individuals who encourage growth, provide constructive feedback, and challenge our thinking promotes continuous progress.

If there is no progress, then there is only stagnancy. Without progress, you may become stagnant, trapped in the same patterns, and unable to move forward. Stagnancy can lead you down the road to a lack of inspiration, motivation, and drive. It can also cause you to feel unfulfilled, bored, and unchallenged. You may become complacent, stuck in the same routines, and unable to respond to changing circumstances. Progress is essential for continuous learning, adaptation, and evolution and is vital for personal and collective development.

Purpose – Plan – Proceed

Maybe you are ready for a change, ready to progress, desiring growth but just not sure where to start or even what to do.

However, to progress, action does need to take place because as I always say, "*you cannot edit a blank page*" and therefore that means you need to start moving. The first thing you want to figure out is the WHAT and then the HOW.

> *You cannot edit a blank page.*

If you are ready for a change and desire growth but are unsure where to start or what to do, taking action is essential to progress. It is necessary that you have a goal and put a plan in place. Setting a clear objective allows you to focus your efforts and determine the necessary steps to achieve it. Developing a plan provides a roadmap to guide your actions and ensure that you stay on track. Taking that first step towards your goal, no matter how small, can ignite momentum and pave the way for further progress and growth. Firstly, lets figure out 'The What' – *you cannot plan unless you know what you are planning for.* This takes us ot the next point *purpose.*

> *You cannot plan unless you know what you are planning for*

Purpose

A purpose is the reason for which something is done or created, or for which something exists. It provides meaning and direction to our actions and efforts. Therefore, in order to be effective, I firmly believe that both purpose and passion need to walk hand in hand. There is a beautiful quote that resonates with me: *"Purpose is the reason you journey. Passion is the fire that lights your way."* So, let us delve into these two powerful aspects that are essential in creating the life you desire.

> *Purpose is the reason you journey. Passion is the fire that lights your way*

Discovering your purpose is a transformative moment when you truly begin to live. It could be centred around your children, leaving a legacy, or serving people you need to help, as is the case for me. Notice that I said, "need to help" rather than "want to help." Your purpose needs to be strong enough to fuel your passion. Purpose and passion are closely related, but they are not quite the same. Your purpose is your WHY, the underlying reason that drives you, while passion is the intense drive and enthusiasm to achieve it.

When purpose and passion align, they create a powerful force that propels you forward on your journey. Your passion fuels your drive to achieve your WHY, while your WHY, or purpose, gives direction and meaning to your passion.

So, I ask you, what is your purpose?

If you're not feeling fulfilled or happy with your life, it may be time to examine your life's purpose. This process of self-reflection can be challenging, and it may lead you to believe that you've wasted your life or lived it the wrong way. But don't worry, it's never too late to create or start living the life you truly deserve - a life that is meaningful and happy.

Have you ever taken the time to explore the things you're passionate about or reflect on your past experiences and challenges? These can be clues to discovering your true purpose. It's often said, "It is more important to know your WHY than your how." Personally, I didn't realise my true purpose until I went through painful experiences. People would often approach me for advice or to talk about their problems, and I never thought much of it. But after going through my own challenges, I realised that I had a natural inclination to guide and support others. This led me down the road of becoming a Mentor, a path I had never considered before. Sometimes, your pain can become your passion. By finding and clarifying your life purpose and core intentions, you can navigate through life with greater focus and clarity. In today's challenging and uncertain times, it is crucial to set clear intentions and develop a refined life purpose. This will make it easier to manage difficult moments.

There are various ways to discover and develop your life purpose and intentions. Many useful resources are available to guide you on this journey of self-discovery. Below, I uncover a few suggestions that can provide direction and inspire you to live a richer, fuller life.

As you explore your life purpose and intentions, start by asking yourself two key questions:

What is most important to me in my life?

What are my deepest values and beliefs?

Your life purpose is typically a single statement that reflects the overall reason you believe you are here. It unveils the greater purpose behind your existence.

Have you ever wondered why you're here in this world?

Many of my clients have lived aimlessly for a long time because they didn't know their purpose, leaving them feeling empty and uncertain about the choices they've made. If you're reading this and can relate, don't worry. It's never too late to discover your purpose, as I have witnessed with a lovely lady I met who started pursuing her writing and speaking career at the age of seventy – Yep 70!

There are various statements, exercises, and questions you can use to help you figure out your purpose, some of which include paying close attention to your heart rather than the calculations of doubt in your mind, listening to your past experiences, evaluating your interests, and noticing what captivates you. Some of these tasks require your undivided attention and deep thought, as the answers may not come easily. This point you definitely do not want to forget, the power of Prayer and listening intentively for Gods response. However, keep in mind that sometimes we discover our purpose along the way and at times the answer may not be as clear as you want it to be, especially when it does not come in the packaging or let me say the way that you anticipated. Joseph I am sure didn't think being sold by his brothers would lead him to his purpose and I definitely had no clue that my traumatic experience would lead me to mine. Therefore keep an open mind!

Discovering your purpose in life can be an incredibly empowering journey. It's all about understanding your passions, values, and the unique gifts you bring to the world. If you're wondering how to unlock your true purpose, here are some helpful ways to guide you on your path:

- When it comes to discovering your purpose, prayer is undoubtedly a powerful tool. Seeking the face of God and asking for answers can provide deep insights and guidance. However, it's important to note as I highlighted before that God's answers may not always come in the way you expect or anticipate. Instead of passively waiting for a clear response, it's crucial to actively take steps and engage in meaningful actions. Many people have found their God-given purpose through serving others. Service can act as a remarkable roadmap, helping you recognise your unique calling and talents. So, let go of the expectation that God will simply drop a Satnav or Waze App from the sky, leading you directly to your purpose. Instead, embrace the journey and actively participate in service and self-discovery. By taking steps towards making a difference and serving others, you'll gradually unfold the path where your purpose resides. Remember, beautiful soul, that the journey to discovering your purpose is multifaceted, and different individuals may find their path in various ways. Keep seeking, keep serving, and trust that God's answers will gently unfold as you actively pursue your calling.

- Explore your passions: Take the time to dive deep into the things that make your heart sing. What activities or causes ignite a fire within you? Pay attention to what resonates with your soul and brings you joy

- It's easy: What do other people find difficult that you do easily? You may often hear people say it to you repeatedly and commend you about it.

- Reflect on your values: Clarify your core values and what truly matters to you. What principles do you hold dear? Aligning your purpose with your values will help you live a more meaningful life.

- Listen to your intuition: Trust your inner voice and intuition. Quiet the noise around you and give yourself space to be still and listen to the whispers of your heart. Your intuition often has valuable insights about your path.

- Seek inspiration: Surround yourself with positive role models and seek inspiration from others who have found their purpose. Read books, listen to podcasts, and attend workshops or seminars that align with your interests. Learning from others can help spark your own ideas.

- Embrace self-discovery: Engage in self-reflection and introspection. Journaling, meditation, and mindfulness practices can help you deepen your self-awareness and uncover your true passions and strengths.

- Experiment and take risks: Don't be afraid to try new things and step outside of your comfort zone. Embrace new experiences, hobbies, or even career changes. Each step forward is an opportunity to learn more about yourself and what truly fulfils you.

- Seek guidance and support: Engage in conversations with mentors, coaches, or trusted friends who can offer guidance and support. Sometimes an outside perspective can provide valuable insights and help you gain clarity. Ask them questions about you.

- Embrace failure (or what I call life's lessons) and learn from setbacks: Remember that setbacks and failures are part of the journey. Embrace them as learning opportunities and let them guide you towards growth and resilience. Your purpose might evolve and change along the way, and that's okay!

- Follow your curiosity: Pay attention to the things that pique your curiosity and lead you down new paths. Sometimes the unexpected can hold hidden clues to your purpose. Stay open-minded and let curiosity be your guide.

- Your Pain - What pains you, those things that you may have experienced or see others go through and it pulls at your heart strings and ignites a fire within you (whether it be excitement or even anger). Pay close attention, that pain may give birth to purpose.

Finding your purpose is a journey that unfolds in its own time. Trust the process, have patience, and believe in yourself. Your purpose is unique to you, and when the time is right, it will reveal itself. Pay careful attention.

Let us take a moment to do a little exercise, you may have seen or done it before but if not before you go any further do it.

The Ikigai Exercise

Ikigai
"a reason for being"

I*   Delight and fullness, but no wealth
II*   Excitement and complacency, but sense of uncertainty
III* Delight and fullness, but no wealth
IV* Excitement and complacency, but sense of uncertainty

Discovering your Ikigai, your "reason for being," is all about finding that deep sense of purpose that makes you excited about why you get out of bed in the morning. To help you navigate this search for your Ikigai, here are 12 questions to consider.

Remember to answer these questions based on your current situation, rather than an idealised one. Some may be a repetition of what I have stated previously, so look for those repeated answers:

- What are you good at?
- Are you useful?
- Have others sought your advice on what you do?
- Do you excel in your workplace or industry?
- Could you become a master in your field with more experience or education?
- What do you love?
- Do you do something you are truly passionate about?
- Can you talk about your work enthusiastically for hours on end?
- Do you feel emotionally connected to the results of your work?
- If money were not a factor, would you still choose the same job?
- What can you offer the world?
- Are you helping to solve a problem?
- Is there a demand in the marketplace for what you have to offer?
- Are people willing to pay (money, attention, or time) for what you provide?

- Will your work still be relevant and needed in the next 10 years?
- What can you be paid for?
- Have you been paid for what you do recently, or are others being paid for similar work?
- Are you currently making a good living from your work, or do you foresee the potential for it in the future?
- Is there a high level of competition in your industry? If yes do you have something else you can bring?
- Do you surpass others who do the same job or offer the same services? By honestly reflecting on these questions and considering how they align with your current situation, you can gain valuable insights into your Ikigai. Remember, your Ikigai is a unique blend of what you are good at, what you love, what the world needs, and what you can be paid for. Embrace the process and trust that the discovery of your Ikigai will lead you to some answers that will enable you to create a more purposeful and fulfilling life. If you find yourself feeling unhappy in your current job, it's important to ask yourself if it aligns with your true calling and purpose. If it doesn't, remember that you have the power to change direction. There are countless opportunities waiting for you to explore.

According to the ikigai method, finding your true purpose is a journey that requires the right intentions. It may take time, perhaps even years or decades, to discover your reason for being. It's important to note that what feels like your life purpose today might not hold the same significance when you re-evaluate it in the future. That's why it's crucial to continuously explore and search for what truly makes you feel engaged and happy.

You owe it to yourself to embark on this journey of self-discovery. *Stop allowing your purpose to be a concubine while other things take first and centre place in your life.* Start looking for what ignites your passion and brings you joy. Remember, your true purpose is out there, waiting for you to uncover it. Embrace the process and trust that with the right intentions, you will eventually find your true calling. When you find your purpose, everything else seems to fade away in the background, excuses and limitations become irrelevant. It's a fulfilling and gratifying experience that is worth the challenges you go through to discover it. So, don't be afraid to embark on the journey of finding your purpose and let it guide you towards a more meaningful and purposeful life.

> *Stop allowing your purpose to be a concubine while other things take first and centre place in your life*

Remember, ladies, your purpose is already within you. Trust yourself, embrace the journey, and know that you have the power to live a life rich with meaning and fulfilment. I'm here cheering you on every step of the way.

Passion is your fuel.

Our passion plays a significant role in helping us reach our highest potential and ignite our purpose, so let's delve deeper into its importance on our journey. As I mentioned earlier, our passion is distinct from our purpose; our purpose is the vehicle, while our passion is the fuel that keeps the vehicle going.

Now, let's explore what it is that you truly want. If you're unsure, now is the perfect time to figure it out. It's astonishing to note that 70% of individuals are not passionate about what they do because they have allowed 'possibility blindness' to reign, causing them to settle for second best. They may think, "My dream or desire is too big and cannot be accomplished, so what else can I do?" *One thing I would like to highlight here, though, is that if the vision isn't so huge that it scares you, then the million-dollar question is – is it really a vision or just another task?* Consequently, you come across talented individuals who are sitting behind an office desk fulfilling someone else's vision, stacking shelves, or working a job they detest. Please don't misunderstand me or hear what I am not saying. I am not saying anything is wrong with these jobs. I am simply saying DO NOT SETTLE. I want to say this though, do not regret or be ungrateful about where you are at right now but do not SETTLE for second best but instead use it as a stepping stone to get to where you need to be. Some settle out of comfort or the fact that it is easier, others start in one avenue with the aim of it being a steppingstone to their purpose and then become complacent and remain as it seems to be the safer option. This is so unfortunate and hence why the graveyard is filled with the ideas and visions that were never given birth to.

> *One thing I would like to highlight here, though, is that if the vision isn't so huge that it scares you, then the million-dollar question is – is it really a vision or just another task?*

True success cannot be achieved if you lack passion for what you do. No matter how well you may be doing in terms of accomplishments, deep down, you'll know whether you are genuinely happy and satisfied. It is up to you to discover what your true calling in life is. Allow me to pose this question to you:

ARE YOU TRULY HAPPY?

ARE YOU FEELING FULFILLED WITH WHAT YOU ARE DOING NOW?

In today's society, individuals face numerous challenges on their journey to finding their place. One of the many issues is excuses, coming up with a million and one reasons as to why your vision or purpose is not possible to execute. The question I pose to you is this: Will you become a story filled with excuses or a story of success?

Even after I discovered my purpose and developed a strong passion for it, I still encountered excuses and stumbled upon obstacles along the way. But here's the thing, your passion will revive you in those deep dark moments, your passion will help to keep your hope alive. It's important not to let setbacks discourage you. Everyone faces challenges when striving to fulfil their purpose. The key difference lies in not allowing those challenges to make you give up. Your purpose will keep you focused, and your passion will reignite your drive. When you are truly passionate about your purpose, you will have the strength to weather any storm as it will keep you motivated and determined.

However, it is worth noting that being passionate about your purpose can come with its own challenges. You may find it difficult to switch off or take a break from pursuing your passion. This can cause burnout and overwhelm at the same time. After all, being so driven that you can't stop can become a downfall. It's important to strike a balance and make time for rest and your personal life. Creating the life you desire requires finding that equilibrium. The power of passion resides within your heart and the recesses of your mind. Whether it's creating your next masterpiece, writing a groundbreaking novel, starting a business, charity, or hosting a captivating event, harnessing the strength of your passion can lead to remarkable results when channelled into your purpose.

Many women long to find their purpose or have any insight into what keeps them ticking even at the worse times in their lives. They yearn for that feeling of excitement and anticipation each morning, they long to hit that level of living a balanced life. It's not uncommon for people to seek flexibility and fulfilment in their work. However, many find themselves stuck in dissatisfying jobs simply to make ends meet. Remember, you always have a choice, even if you cannot yet see the path clearly. With support and determination, you can pave the way towards creating and enjoying the life you desire.

Do not become a murderer of your dreams and vision by settling for less. Living passionately in alignment with your purpose is like lighting a candle in the darkness - it gives purpose and meaning to your existence. Within you lies a unique gift, a talent or ability that sets you apart. It may be something that comes effortlessly to you but proves challenging for others. However, you may not have fully recognised this gift or allowed excuses to hinder your progress. Today, I want to encourage you to take a chance on yourself and unleash your full potential by taking that first step. Remember, every extraordinary journey begins with a single step, and that step could be all it takes to let your light shine brightly.

> ### *Do not become a murderer of your dreams and vision by settling for less*

I once came across a quote that deeply resonated with me, and I believe it will inspire you also. Anita Roddick once said, "*If you think you are too small to make an impact, try going to bed with a mosquito in the room.*" These words serve as a reminder that even the smallest beings can create a significant impact. So, don't underestimate the power of your unique gift. Embrace it, nurture it, and allow it to guide you as you make your mark on the world.

> ### *If you think you are too small to make an impact, try going to bed with a mosquito in the room.*

Believe in yourself and take that first step, knowing that within you lies the potential to create a meaningful impact. Don't let excuses hold you back any longer. It's time to let your light shine and share your gift with the world.

> *You are the light of the world. A city set on a hill cannot be hidden. Nor do people light a lamp and put it under a basket, but on a stand, and it gives light to all in the house. In the same way, let your light shine before others, so that they may see your good works and give glory to your Father who is in heaven.*
>
> Matt 5:14-16

Planning

Effective planning is a crucial strategy for achieving your goals. Imagine wanting to reach a particular destination at a specific time, but lacking directions, knowledge of transportation options, or awareness of costs. You wake up early on the day of the journey, pack your essentials, but the chances of getting derailed, lost, missing the destination entirely or arriving late are highly likely. This scenario mirrors the experiences of so many women who remain busy throughout the year, only to realise by year-end that they have made little or no progress towards their goals. Have you been there? Because I know I have.

So, what exactly is a plan?

A plan is a detailed proposal that outlines how to accomplish something, representing an intention or decision about one's actions. The first step in the planning process is to consider what you want to create and achieve. From there, you formulate a plan that delineates the necessary steps and commit to following through.

While it may seem straightforward and easy, the reality is that executing plans successfully can be a challenge. How often have you made plans that failed to materialise? Consider something as simple as planning your day - how many times have you created a schedule but failed to adhere to it, resulting in unachieved desired outcomes for the day? I have worked with so many women that I gave the task of mapping their daily time management and some were gobsmacked by the amount of unproductive hours they had, whether it be down to the constant scrolling on Instagram and the many unfruitful short girlie chats that they accommodated during the week which if put together amounts to hours, or the many Netflix binges on the sofa in between work and they would tell me boldly when given a task that they don't have time. (I do have my Netflix binges at times so not knocking it but its during my me time, not when it's execution time.)

Do you want the truth?

It is not that you don't have time but more about how serious you are about achieving your goals.

How intentional are you?

This highlights the importance of not only creating a plan but also implementing it effectively. It requires discipline, commitment, and adaptability. Successful planning involves understanding your priorities, breaking down goals into actionable steps, anticipating distractions, obstacles, and being flexible enough to adjust the plan as needed. By doing so, you increase your chances of achieving the desired results and maximising your potential. Remember, a plan is more than just a list of tasks to be completed; it serves as a roadmap that guides you towards your goals. Embrace the planning process, stay focused, and be willing to adjust along the way.

With effective planning, you can overcome obstacles, make meaningful progress, and unleash your full potential. Planning for your life is undoubtedly important, but it's essential not to become overly rigid. Just like in any aspect of life, balance is key. While having a well-thought-out plan provides direction, helps you prioritise, and enables you to make the right choices at the right time, it's also crucial to embrace the present moment.

For a significant period of my life, I had no concrete plans in place. As a result, I found myself aimlessly drifting, despite working hard and being busy. It seemed normal at the time, but deep down I knew I was falling short. It took me a while to realise that I was constantly busy and distracted by the wrong things, and so I made some necessary changes.

It's important to recognise that everyone has their own unique plan for their life, based on the goals they want to accomplish. Some women may appear content and free-spirited, with no apparent desire for traditional achievements. While this may not align with your plan, it could be their intentional choice. However, there are also those who have no plan at all, simply living day to day with no thought for the future, and you must be careful if you have them in your circle, that they don't cause you to drift.

In life, we all have choices to make. I've encountered clients who claim to have a plan, only to present me with a list of things they want to have in the future on a sheet of paper – A WISH. While setting goals is part of the plan, it's not the plan itself. When I ask them about the steps they'll take to achieve those goals, they often draw a blank. They haven't thought through the path to reach their targets, and this is a common and critical mistake.

Your goals are indeed a component of your plan, as they represent the desired end results of your achievements. However, a comprehensive plan goes beyond listing goals. It involves mapping out the steps, strategies, and actions required to bring those goals to fruition. It involves understanding how each objective connects and contributes to the overarching plan. So, while planning is crucial, remember to strike a balance. Embrace the present moment, adapt to unforeseen circumstances, and remain flexible along the way. A well-crafted plan, supported by actionable steps, will provide the foundation for achievements that align with your vision for a fulfilling life.

Setting goals is often compared to a football game. I don't know if you are a football watcher or fan (I am an Arsenal fan – don't hate), the aim of the game is to score the most goals. However, there is much more to the game than just scoring goals. Before a goal is scored, there is a whole play that unfolds on the pitch. It involves following rules, utilising tactics, and considering various factors. Similarly, in having a goal, there are certain plays, strategies, and setups you have to put in place to get that ball in the back of the net. While setting goals is important, it is equally essential to have a plan for executing the necessary actions to achieve those goals. Starting a journey without a plan of how to reach your destination is unwise. Without a plan, you may soon find yourself wondering about the next step to take.

Surprisingly, in today's society, many people have wish lists rather than goal sheets. For instance, imagine a woman in August who includes "giving birth to a baby before the end of the year" on her so-called goal sheet. This lacks logic. While it is reasonable to aspire to become pregnant, stating a specific date for giving birth is not realistic. It may result in bringing a seriously premature baby into the world who may not even survive. Similarly, treating wishes as goals can lead to premature and unsatisfactory outcomes.

This highlights the importance of goal setting and how to approach it effectively.

The SMART goals strategy is a popular approach to goal setting.

SPECIFIC – Ensure that your goal is well-defined, clear, and easily understood.

MEASURABLE – Make sure your goal is attainable and establish a timeline for achieving it. This will allow you to track your progress and recognise when you have successfully reached your goal.

ATTAINABLE – Focus on creating actionable goals that are agreed upon and do not constantly change due to challenges. By doing so, you can maintain a sense of direction and stay motivated.

RELEVANT – Always have a clear reason or purpose behind your goal. Ensure that it aligns with your available time, resources, and knowledge to increase your chances of success.

TIME-BOUND – Differentiate your goal from a mere wish by setting a specific timeframe to accomplish it. Providing yourself with enough time allows for proper planning and execution.

In addition, it's important to write down your goals and visually display them. You can do this through a list, vision board, or a dream book. Find a method that works best for you and visualise your goals daily. Did you notice what I said? Vision board. It can keep motivating you to put in the work. I am not talking about trying to look at it long enough to see if you can manifest it without doing the work or positioning yourself to receive it. I know many have done that and are still waiting as the years pass by.

While keeping goals in your mind may seem sufficient, it's crucial to have them clearly written down. This way, you can plan the necessary steps to achieve them. Habakkuk 2:2 *"Write the vision; make it plain on tablets, so he may run who reads it."*

Goal setting is a powerful process that helps you create the life you desire and turn your vision into reality. It allows you to make informed choices about your future and know exactly what you want to achieve and where to focus your efforts.

Setting goals involves considering different levels:

1. Start by considering what you want to achieve in your lifetime. These long-term goals offer a wide perspective to steer your decision-making process.
2. Divide your lifetime goals into smaller objectives that you must accomplish to attain those larger goals.
3. Develop a plan that incorporates weekly, monthly, and yearly milestones essential for reaching the previously mentioned two levels.

HABAKKUK 2:2
"Write the vision; make it plain on tablets, so he may run who reads it."

I believe goals should cover important areas of your life in a balanced manner. Why? Because true success is about having a balanced life. It's not worth being successful in business if its causing your relationships with your spouse and/or children to fail. If you're not careful, you might find yourself celebrating victories alone. Some areas that are commonly covered include family, finances, career, health, education, leisure, and business.

By setting balanced goals and understanding where you're headed, you can create a meaningful and fulfilling life.

Setting goals is important, but it's not enough if you don't know how to stay on track. That's where having a plan comes in. Once you have your goals, you need to establish a process that involves reviewing, updating, and maintaining a daily to-do list. Life's circumstances may require you to modify or change priorities but having a plan in place will help you adapt and stay on track. Without a plan, it's hard to make effective modifications or adjustments, and this is where effective scheduling plays a crucial role. Some people fall into the trap of making excuses and wanting to quit when they face challenges because they don't have a plan they can modify or reorganise. They end up with a life filled with endless tasks but little accomplishments. However, working smarter instead of longer is what most people desire. Having the right plan in place can make this possible for you.

As Jim Rohn once said, *"Everything you do is a link in the chain of events that will lead you to your final destination."* Successful people are aware of each step they need to take towards their goals and have the discipline to follow through. Your direction, activities, and discipline are all key components of your plan for success.

One crucial point I would like to emphasise is that it's important not to jump into the activities on your to-do list until you have a clear understanding of what your plan is aiming to achieve. This will help you determine if your actions are aligned with your goals. There are many things that can distract you from sticking to your plan on a daily basis, things that you may not have prepared for or have allowed to get in the way without realising it. For example, constantly checking emails, being bombarded with social media notifications, and receiving numerous phone calls can all be distractions that consume a significant portion of your day. I'm not suggesting that you completely isolate yourself from the world, but there should be times when you choose to be focused and dedicate uninterrupted time to achieve your goals. This may involve switching off your phone for a while, scheduling specific times to check your emails, and practicing discipline in order to prioritise your goals.

> *Everything you do is a link in the chain of events that will lead you to your final destination.*

Whilst writing this book, I realised that the deadline I had set to publish was quickly approaching, and I had allowed many distractions to take place – I started to have days where everything was turned off. I realised that I was in motion to give birth and could not allow anything in the labour room to distract me from pushing and successfully delivering myself of this baby. We've all experienced that situation where we start on one thing and end up getting side-tracked by random searches and scrolling through unrelated topics. I'm sure you can relate. It may not always be with technology, but it can happen with even those in your home and so removing yourself from the space of your home can also sometimes be a gamechanger.

Here's the thing, in the end, you are the one responsible for planning your own success.

I can provide you with tips and ideas, but ultimately, you are the one who will determine what works best for you in planning your own success. Yes, you can pray but you still have to be the one to obey Gods command and action the steps directed – even when you don't understand how it is going to work. *Faith without works is dead*

For me, what works is breaking down my goals into major, monthly, sub-goals, and micro-goals. I use a weekly sheet as a reminder of the overall purpose of the steps I'm taking or the tasks that need to be executed. I also find it helpful to use a diary/calendar for effective daily planning. If I notice that I am unable to achieve my monthly goals, I analyse my weekly and daily routines to identify and eliminate any issues that may be hindering my progress. It's crucial to honestly assess how I use my hours throughout the day. Often, time management becomes a factor, which involves addressing the distractions I mentioned earlier.

Creating a time management sheet and meticulously recording how I spend every single minute of my day can be eye-opening. It helps me identify how much time I may be wasting on activities that don't align with my goals or monthly targets. Once I recognise the common factors that consume my time, I schedule my day by allocating specific durations to the tasks I need to accomplish and stick to the schedule until they are completed. It's important to take ownership of your life and recognise that you are responsible for the outcomes. The progress you make toward your goals is measured by the steps you take and the efforts you put forth. Take the time to identify the obstacles that need to be overcome in order to achieve your goals.

Be wise, yes take time out to learn from others but don't spend hours on social media watching and reminiscing over the life of another, because whilst you are watching they are building, and you are diminishing with anxiety from comparison. Stop dreaming and start implanting so that you can bring the dreams to life, do not sit waiting for the perfect time to come, because you might end up waiting to your grave.

I'd like to share some effective planning tips that can help you achieve your goals:

1. **Clearly define your objectives**: Have a clear understanding of what you want to achieve.

2. **Write down and understand your action steps**: Document the specific actions you need to take to make progress.

3. **Break it down**: Segment your actions into smaller sub-goals or micro-goals for easier implementation.

4. **Minimise distractions**: Create a plan to eliminate or manage the distractions that can hinder your progress.

5. **Self-analysis**: Continuously evaluate yourself at each step. Ask yourself if you can do more and if your actions are leading you closer to your target.

6. **Work towards the next step**: Always have clarity about what comes next and set a schedule or timeline accordingly.

7. **Address challenges**: Understand your challenges and develop strategies to overcome them.

8. **Set deadlines and prioritise**: Establish deadlines for your tasks and prioritise them based on their importance and urgency.

9. **Eliminate excuses and procrastination**: Adopt a mindset of tackling the most difficult task first, just as Mark Twain

suggested. This can help you overcome the tendency to make excuses or delay important work.

10. **Take breaks and recharge**: Remember to press the stop button occasionally and take time to pause. Allow yourself some dedicated "me time" to relax and recharge.

I hope these tips prove helpful to you, just as they have helped me. Now, it's time to put your plan into action and make great things happen!

The permanent pause

I hope this chapter has blessed you with some nuggets to help you move forward on your journey. As I close off this chapter the one thing that came to mind as the best point to end on is what I call the 'permanent pause.' I chose to end with this because it is one of the great enemies of progress and a common one that prevents many women from taking action, especially taking the first step.

If you were wondering what the permanent pause is, let me put your mind to rest.

Perfectionism

Ah, perfectionism. It's a topic I'm all too familiar with, and one that affects many ambitious women. Perfectionism is the belief that everything must be flawless and without error. It's that constant striving for flawlessness in every aspect of our lives, from our work to our appearance and beyond. While it may seem like a noble pursuit, it can hinder progress and keep you from reaching your full potential. Perfectionism can prevent women from living up to their best potential in several ways. First, it can lead to an overwhelming **fear of failure**. When we set impossibly high standards for ourselves, we become afraid to take risks or try new things because we're scared of making mistakes. This fear can paralyse us and keep us from seizing opportunities for growth and success.

Secondly, perfectionism can lead to an **excessive focus on our flaws and shortcomings**. We become hyper-critical of ourselves, constantly finding faults, and never feeling 'good enough'. This **negative self-talk** can chip away at your **self-esteem** and **confidence**, leaving you **feeling unworthy of pursuing your dreams and passions**.

Additionally, the pursuit of perfection can be incredibly **time-consuming and exhausting**. We become so fixated on getting everything just right that **we neglect other important aspects of our lives**, such as self-care, relationships, and personal fulfilment. **We sacrifice our own well-being in pursuit of an unattainable ideal**, which ultimately leaves us feeling **burnt** out and **unfulfilled**.

Perfectionism also **robs you of the joy and satisfaction** that comes from embracing imperfections and learning from your mistakes. It's through our mistakes and failures that we grow, learn, and become better versions of ourselves. By striving for perfection, **we deny ourselves the opportunity to fail forward** and discover our true strengths and capabilities.

But fear not, my dear Eikonic Woman! There is a way to break free from the grip of perfectionism and unleash your full potential. It starts with practicing self-compassion and embracing your imperfections. Remember that you are human, and it's okay to make mistakes. Accept that perfection is an unattainable goal and shift your focus towards progress and growth instead. It is important to give yourself permission to take risks, make mistakes, and learn from them.

You are capable of incredible things, embrace your imperfections, step into your power, and live a life that's authentically yours. I am here to support you every step of the way. Remember, I have said this before, you cannot edit a blank page, so how do you think you can perfect something you have not yet started? Take the step and edit as you go along, start writing and stop expecting God to bless what you have not yet executed. God will multiply what you bring to him, so the bread and fish might not be enough, but bring it, it is something to work from. Perfectionism leads to procrastination and procrastination manifests into the permanent pause. Do not let permanent pause alter what the dash between your date of birth and date of death on your head stone when you leave this earth will say or not say about you.

Podcast

https://qrco.de/bf6o5Y

- *Have a Business Concept*
- *Who is your Ideal Client?*
- *Content that sells*
- *It's time to Construct*
- *Go down the right Channel*
- *Creating a Memorable Brand Identity*

Turning Your Purpose into Profit

CHAPTER THREE

Turning Your Purpose into Profit

"Return on investment can only happen when you have first invested."

MICHELLE WATSON

This chapter, I believe some of you may have a conflict with or may even want to skip, purely because you have a red alert or exclamation sign pulsing in your head. The question that has found its way to your thoughts and even out of your lips is, "Should I really be charging for my purpose, something God gave me the ability freely to do?"

You pose such a profound question: Should your purpose be offered for free since it was bestowed upon you by the divine? It's a thought that resonates deeply with the essence of who you are and the values you hold dear.

So, let's explore this together.

While your purpose is indeed a gift from God, let us consider this perspective: What if, instead of viewing it as a transaction of free service, we think of it as a calling to share your unique brilliance with the world, while also honouring the value it brings to others and yourself?

Your purpose is a beacon of light that can inspire and uplift those around you. It has the power to transform lives, create positive change, and contribute to the greater good. And while sharing your purpose may be an act of love and service, it is also essential to recognise that there is value in the wisdom, skills, and expertise you bring forth. You deserve to thrive! Think about all you have invested – time, energy, and resources – into honing your skills, building your expertise, and nurturing your purpose. If I were to do that calculation, you would be seeing a good number of zeros. I have invested heavily in my development – mentors, programmes, events, books – and if we then throw in my experience of being the guinea pig to save you from making the mistakes I made and expediting your process based on my experience knowledge – PRICELESS!

It is perfectly aligned to honour both your divine calling and your personal growth by offering your gifts through avenues that generate abundance and sustainability.

Creating a harmonious balance between sharing your purpose freely and receiving financial reward honours the beautiful reciprocity between your soul's calling and your earthly needs. By valuing your unique gifts, you empower yourself to continue on the path of growth, expansion, and creating a positive impact in the lives of others. So, my sister, embrace the duality of your purpose. Share it with love, generosity, and a giving heart, while also recognising the value it holds and seeking ways to create a sustainable and prosperous life that aligns with your divine calling. When I first embarked on my journey as a business mentor, I faced a challenging internal battle that persisted for far too long. I found myself questioning, "How dare I charge for something that was given to me by God?" The discomfort I felt was palpable. Even when I mustered the courage to charge, I did so at the lowest cost possible, even if it meant putting myself out of pocket – a decision that, in hindsight, seems rather baffling. Reflecting on that period, I can't help but wonder what planet I was on. How could any business run or be sustained with such undercharging practices? It was during my first session with my business mentor that reality struck. I was asked if I was crazy, as it was evident that I was undervaluing my services. Even with my mentors guidance, I still found it difficult to break free from the confines of undercharging.

But my second business mentor was not going to let me continue down that path. By this time, I had experienced significant personal and business growth. I had invested in my own development, gaining invaluable knowledge and honing my expertise. In essence, I was now offering so much more than before, yet still charging the low rates.

I'll never forget the day I was challenged to add another zero, in fact, add another two zeros to my pricing. The mere thought of it sent my heart pounding. However, I summoned the courage to take that leap of faith. And let me tell you, I never looked back. When I confidently presented my new fees to a client for their 1:1 session, the sound of my bank account "pinging" was music to my ears. It was a moment of affirmation that I had embraced my worth, recognised the value of my purpose, and had the courage to charge accordingly.

This transformational experience taught me an invaluable lesson: I must never undervalue myself or my expertise. Charging what I'm truly worth allows me to serve my clients at the highest level while also sustaining and growing my own business. More importantly, it allowed me to give back – let's do the math for a hot minute, how many people can you help if you cannot even help yourself? God has blessed me, and I have been able to use what I have received to also bless others who are less fortunate, that for me says it all. I share this so that you realise that I know all too well the internal battle you're facing. The struggle between wanting to charge clients for your purpose and the fear of charging too much. But let me share a powerful truth with you: That battle is not about charging clients; it's about recognising your true self-worth and value. Your purpose is a remarkable gift, one that you have nurtured, developed, and honed over time. It holds the power to transform lives and bring immense value to those who benefit from it. It's time to acknowledge the depth of this value and honour your self-worth.

Charging for your purpose doesn't diminish its significance or your integrity; it affirms the immense worth you bring to the table. By recognising the value of your services, you create a harmonious exchange that allows both you and your clients to thrive. Its crucial to take a step back and reflect on what you are truly bringing to the table. Consider the unique experiences, expertise, and wisdom you possess. Understand the impact your purpose has on others and the meaningful difference it makes in their lives.

Remember, my extraordinary friend, as I previously mentioned you are not just charging for your purpose, but for the time, energy, resources, and investments you have dedicated to developing your skills and knowledge. You deserve to be compensated fairly for the value you bring to others. Now is the time to release any limiting beliefs or fears that have kept you from recognising your self-worth. Embrace the realisation that your purpose is worthy of being valued both monetarily and energetically. Allow yourself to step into a space of empowerment, abundance, and receiving what you deserve.

So now, I encourage you to reflect on your own journey and recognise the value of your purpose. Don't allow fear or a sense of unworthiness to prevent you from charging what you deserve. Embrace the confidence to add those zeros and experience the abundance that comes when you fully honour the value you bring. May your purpose continue to shine brightly, attracting those who can benefit from your profound wisdom and guidance. You are a vessel of divine light, and by embracing both the spiritual and practical aspects of your purpose, you have the power to uplift countless souls and create a ripple effect of empowerment and abundance. Have unwavering faith in your journey and anticipation for all the possibilities.

Is it possible to turn my purpose into a profitable business?

Absolutely! Your purpose is not just a beautiful dream to be admired from afar; it holds the potential to be a source of both deep fulfilment and financial abundance.

In today's world, where authenticity and passion are prized more than ever, there is an incredible opportunity for you to align your purpose with profit. When you tap into what truly lights you up inside and channel that energy into a business or endeavour, the possibilities are boundless. But here's the secret, my ladies: turning your purpose into profit is not just about making money. It's about creating a sustainable and joyful life where you wake up excited to pursue your dreams each day. It's about having the freedom to share your unique gifts with the world while reaping the rewards that come with it and trust me the rewards will come, once you have the right attitude, advice and take action.

To turn your purpose into profit, begin by exploring your true passions and understanding how they can serve others. Ask yourself: What am I most passionate about? Which we covered earlier. What skills, knowledge, or experiences can you offer that will bring value to others? By discovering the intersection between your purpose and the needs of the world, you will uncover your pathway to profitability.

From there, my lovely Eikonic Woman, it's all about taking inspired action. Create a solid business plan, build a strong personal brand that reflects your purpose and values, and connect with your target audience authentically. Be open to learning, refining your approach, and seeking support and guidance when needed. Remember, success is not a solo journey – it thrives in community and shared experiences.

The pursuit of turning your purpose into profit is a journey that many aspire to embark on - aligning their passions with financial success. And you know what? It's absolutely within your reach!

To turn it into profit, you'll need to combine your passion with strategic thinking and practical action. Here are a few steps to guide you on this exciting journey:

1. **Clarify Your Vision**: Take the time to get crystal clear on what you want to achieve. Visualise your ideal outcome and set ambitious yet attainable goals. Let this vision fuel your motivation and determination.

2. **Identify Your Market**: Who are the people that can benefit from your unique gifts and offerings? Get to know your target audience, understand their needs, and tailor your products or services to cater to them.

3. **Understand Your Value**: Recognise the unique value you bring to the table. What makes you different from others in your field? (USP – Unique Selling Point) Highlight your strengths, skills, and expertise, and use them to your

advantage. Embrace your authenticity because that's what attracts people to you.

4. **Invest in Yourself**: Cultivate a growth mindset and continuously develop your skills and knowledge. Attend workshops, read books, and surround yourself with mentors who can guide you on your journey. The more you invest in yourself, the more valuable you become.

5. **Build a Strong Personal Brand**: Your personal brand is what sets you apart. Showcase your expertise, maintain a strong online presence, and connect with your audience through engaging content. Be consistent and authentic in your messaging and let your purpose shine through every interaction.

6. **Monetise Your Passion**: Explore different avenues to monetise your service or product. This could include offering digital products, creating online courses, or coaching programs, hosting workshops or events, or even leveraging your expertise through consulting or speaking engagements. Find the avenue that aligns best with your strengths and values.

Remember, that the journey of turning your purpose into profit is not always linear. It may involve detours, setbacks, and moments of self-doubt. But with perseverance and resilience, you will find your way. Surround yourself with a supportive community of like-minded women who uplift and inspire each other along this shared path.

I have complete faith in your ability to transform your purpose into profit, embrace your strengths, follow your passion, and believe in the incredible value you have to offer the world.

You need to have a Business *Concept*

Now, we are going to be diving deeper into the business element of things and if you didn't take notes, you might want to start now.

We will be looking at the six C's that I cover in my Profitable Business Blueprint module within the Eikonic Women Quadrant. The first C is Concept. What do I mean by Concept? I mean creating a solid business plan, a plan for not only business success but one that will get you closer to living the life you desire. I highlight this fact because most tend to create their life around their business instead of the business around their life.

A business concept is a fundamental idea or proposition that forms the core foundation of a potential business. It encapsulates the essence of the business and articulates its unique value proposition in the marketplace. A well-developed business concept outlines the product or service, target market, competitive advantage, and a strategy for delivering customer value. The first step in developing a business concept is identifying a problem or need in the market that the business aims to address - a problem that you can solve based on your studies, experience, or capabilities. This could be a gap in the market that has not yet been fulfilled or an opportunity to improve upon existing offerings. Please do not fall into the common trap of saying 'someone is doing that already.' Someone may be, however, you may have a unique way of delivery, something your competitor doesn't have - a USP (Unique Selling Point). We are all unique in our own way. We could both say the same thing, but it is delivered and received differently.

A unique selling point (USP) refers to the distinct element or feature of a product, service, or business that sets it apart from competitors and gives it a competitive advantage in the market. It is a compelling reason why customers should choose a particular offering over alternatives. A strong USP enhances brand identity, attracts customers, and drives business success.

To develop a USP, it is essential to thoroughly understand the target market and identify their needs, desires, and pain points. By understanding customers' preferences and motivations, a business can tailor its USP to align with their values and provide a relevant, differentiated solution.

Here are some characteristics of a powerful unique selling point:

1. **Differentiation**: A USP should clearly differentiate a business or product from competitors. It highlights what makes it unique and why customers should choose it over alternatives.

2. **Value Proposition**: A USP should clearly communicate the unique value that the product or service provides to customers. It addresses a specific problem or need and articulates how the offering delivers superior benefits.

3. **Uniqueness**: A USP should be genuinely distinctive and difficult for competitors to imitate. It could be a proprietary technology, a specialised skill set, a unique feature, or a one-of-a-kind approach to solving a problem.

4. **Focused**: A USP should be concise, focused, and easily understood. It should grab the attention of customers and clearly communicate the key benefit that sets it apart.

5. **Authenticity**: A USP should be aligned with the business's ethos and values. It should genuinely reflect the business's strengths, capabilities, and commitment to customer satisfaction.

Remember, a powerful USP is not just a clever marketing slogan or tagline; it is the essence of what sets a product, service, or business apart in the market. By crafting a compelling USP, businesses can effectively communicate their value proposition, attract customers, and create a unique space in the competitive landscape.

For instance, you could be a hairdresser, and yes, there are many around, but then you could be a mobile hairdresser, going to your clients' home instead of them coming to you. This will then allow you to charge premium rates, especially if you can deliver at a high quality. Look at what competitors or potential competitors are doing and see what unique selling point you could bring to the table.

The business concept then takes form by proposing a solution to the problem or need, and you putting your unique spin on it.

One common mistake that I have seen some of my clients make before they come to work with me is starting a business and neglecting to establish a solid business concept. A clear and well-defined idea forms the foundation for a successful venture. Without it, businesses can face challenges in differentiating themselves from competitors, attracting customers, and achieving long-term success. A solid business concept encapsulates the essence of the business and serves as a guiding principle for decision-making, strategic planning, and brand development. A strong business concept articulates the value that the proposed offering will bring to customers. It outlines the key features, benefits, and advantages of the product or service, distinguishing it from competitors and compelling customers to choose it over alternatives. This value proposition should clearly demonstrate how the business concept meets the needs and desires of the target market. Furthermore, a successful business concept considers the target market, understanding their demographics, preferences, and behaviours. By identifying and understanding the target audience, the business can customise its offerings and marketing strategies to effectively reach and engage potential customers.

Competitive advantage (USP) is an important element of a business concept. It involves identifying what sets the business apart from competitors and why customers should choose the proposed offering over alternatives. This could be through factors such as superior quality, cost-effectiveness, innovative features, exceptional customer service, or a unique selling proposition that cannot be easily replicated by competitors.

Lastly, the business concept should outline a strategy for delivering customer value and generating revenue. This includes considerations such as pricing strategies, distribution channels, marketing and promotional tactics, and a plan for attracting and retaining customers.

In summary, a business concept is the fundamental idea or proposition that forms the basis of a potential business idea. It outlines the product or service, target market, competitive advantage, and strategy for delivering customer value. A strong business concept sets the stage for development, growth, and success in the competitive landscape of the business world. This is the first step of mapping out your purpose to turn it into a business, looking at what need it can serve as a solution to, and maybe you cannot see it or are unsure that it can be monetised, but that's where mentors come into play as they may be able to see what you cannot – it does not mean it is not possible.

A well-crafted business plan will provide a roadmap for you as a entrepreneur, guiding you through each stage of your entrepreneurial journey. It helps clarify the business's vision, mission, and target audience, and sets clear goals and timelines for achieving them.

Additionally, having a business concept assists in identifying potential challenges and risks, allowing you to devise contingency plans. It also plays a crucial role in attracting investors, lenders, and potential partners, as it demonstrates your preparedness, professionalism, and commitment to your business idea. By creating a solid concept you can increase your chances of success, make informed decisions, and navigate the ever-changing business landscape with confidence.

Know who your Ideal *Client* is

The next C is Clients – (KYC)Know Your Client. What do I mean by knowing your client? I mean having a deep understanding of the specific group of people who are most likely to benefit from your products or services. It involves gathering detailed information about their demographics, psychographics, preferences, behaviours, and needs. By knowing your ideal client, you can tailor your marketing efforts, product development, and customer experience to effectively meet their specific needs and preferences.

When you know your ideal client, you are aware of:

1. **Demographics**: This includes information such as age, gender, geographic location, education, occupation, and income level. Understanding these demographics helps you segment and target your marketing efforts effectively.

2. **Psychographics**: This refers to the attitudes, values, interests, and lifestyle choices of your ideal client. Knowing their psychographics helps you connect with them on a deeper level and understand what motivates their purchasing decisions.

3. **Preferences and Behaviour's**: Understanding your ideal client's preferences and behaviours enables you to create

products or services that align with their specific wants and needs. This may include factors like preferred communication channels, buying habits, and product/service specifications.

4. **Pain Points and Challenges**: Knowing the pain points and challenges your ideal clients face allows you to develop targeted solutions. By addressing their specific needs, you can position your business as the best option to help them overcome their challenges.

5. **Goals and Aspirations**: Understanding the goals and aspirations of your ideal clients helps you tailor your messaging and positioning. By highlighting how your products or services can help them achieve their desired outcomes, you can create a strong connection and motivate them to choose your business.

In essence, knowing your ideal client means intimately understanding who they are, what they want, and how you can provide value to them. This knowledge guides your marketing strategies, product development, customer service, and overall business decisions, allowing you to serve your target audience more effectively and differentiate yourself from competitors.

When you have a clear understanding of who your ideal client is, you can create targeted marketing campaigns, develop products or services that meet their specific needs, and provide a superior customer experience. To effectively know your ideal client, you need to conduct thorough market research. This involves gathering demographic data, psychographic information, and insights into their preferences, behaviours, and challenges. By analysing this data, you can identify common characteristics and patterns that define your target audience. Creating buyer personas is a helpful tool in understanding your ideal client. These personas are detailed profiles that represent your target customers, including their demographics, characteristics, motivations, goals, and challenges. This exercise helps you visualise and empathise with your ideal clients, allowing you to develop strategies that resonate with them.

Knowing your ideal client enables targeted marketing efforts. With a clear understanding of their preferences, pain points, and aspirations, you can craft messages and choose marketing channels that effectively reach and engage your target audience. By tailoring your marketing campaigns to your ideal client, you increase the likelihood of capturing their attention and converting them into loyal customers. Additionally, understanding your ideal client helps you develop products or services that meet their specific needs. By aligning your offerings with their preferences and solving their pain points, you create a more compelling value proposition. This differentiation sets you apart from competitors and fosters customer loyalty and satisfaction.

Providing a superior customer experience is another advantage of knowing your ideal client. By understanding their preferences, communication styles, and expectations, you can personalise your interactions, communications, and support to better meet their needs. This tailored approach enhances customer satisfaction, fosters brand loyalty, and increases the likelihood of repeat business and positive word-of-mouth recommendations. Furthermore, knowing your ideal client allows for efficient resource allocation. Instead of trying to target a broad audience, focusing your efforts and resources on reaching the right people maximises the effectiveness of your marketing campaigns and utilisation of resources. This strategic approach ensures a better return on investment and allows for more efficient use of your time, money, and energy.

To keep it brief I always tell my clients to focus on their clients NDP (NEEDS – DESIRES – PAIN POINTS) By investing time and effort into understanding your ideal client and their NDP you can position your business for long-term success and growth.

5 easy steps to start

- Create your ideal avatar
- Give them a name, age, character, interests etc.
- Make note of what their NDP's are
- Where are they now? (Point A) Where do they want to be? (Point B) How can you get them across the bridge from point A-B
- Conduct thorough Market research.

Mapping the landscape through market research enables you to make informed decisions and shape your business strategy accordingly. It helps you determine the viability of your business idea, set realistic goals, and identify the target market segments that offer the highest potential for monetisation and growth. Armed with this knowledge, you can create compelling value propositions, refine your marketing messages, and position yourself as a competitive player in the market. Mapping the landscape through market research is an essential step in understanding the market dynamics and identifying business opportunities. It helps you gain insights into your target audience, competition, industry trends, and customer needs. By conducting thorough market research, you can make informed decisions, tailor your strategies, and position your business for success in a competitive marketplace.

The power of your *Content*

I am talking about Creating a Memorable Brand Identity through your content. Now, what does that look like? Creating a memorable brand identity is about more than just a catchy logo or a catchy tagline. It's about crafting authentic and compelling content and a story that resonates with your target audience, evokes emotions, and leaves a lasting impression. Your brand identity reflects who you are as a business and what you stand for. It's the promise you make to your customers and the values you uphold.

To create a memorable brand identity, start by defining your brand's purpose and values. What is the driving force behind your business? What do you believe in? Clarifying your purpose and values will help you establish a strong foundation on which to build your brand.

As I stated before, knowing who your target audience is and what they desire is very relevant to creating a strong and effective brand. Understanding your audience on a deep level allows you to tailor your messaging and brand experience to resonate with them authentically. By speaking directly to their needs and desires, you can create a strong emotional connection that sets your brand apart. Consistency is key when it comes to building a memorable brand identity. Ensure that all aspects of your brand, from visual elements like logos and colours to your tone of voice and messaging, are consistent across all touchpoints. This consistency builds trust and recognition, making it easier for your audience to remember and identify your brand. Another essential aspect of creating a memorable brand identity is storytelling. People connect with stories on a deeper level, so use your brand's story to captivate your audience and communicate your values and mission. Share the journey that led to the creation of your business, the challenges you overcame, and the impact you aim to make in the world. Invite your audience to be part of that story and show them how they can align with your brand.

Lastly, engage and involve your audience in building your brand identity. Encourage them to share their experiences, stories, and feedback. Recognise and celebrate their achievements and contributions to building your brand. By fostering a sense of community and shared success, you create a loyal following and transform customers into brand advocates who proudly represent your business. Creating a memorable brand identity takes time and effort, but the rewards are immeasurable. When you establish a brand that resonates with your audience, connects emotionally, and leaves a lasting impression, you create a powerful asset that sets you apart from your competition.

When it comes to creating content, authenticity is paramount. In a world saturated with brands vying for attention, being genuine and true to yourself is what will set you apart. Embrace your unique qualities and let them shine through in every aspect of your brand. When you show up as your authentic self, you attract like-minded individuals who resonate with your values and connect with your mission. Consistency is also key and extends beyond just visual elements. While having a visually cohesive brand is important, it's equally crucial to maintain consistency in your brand's personality, values, and voice. Your brand should have a consistent tone and language across all platforms and communications. This builds trust and reliability, keeping your brand at the forefront of your audience's minds.

The other key element is emotional engagement; this is a powerful tool. People remember content that makes them feel something. Find ways to establish an emotional connection with your audience. Tug at their heartstrings with inspiring stories, evoke their curiosity through thought-provoking content, and offer support and encouragement in their journey. When you connect with your audience on an emotional level, they become not just customers but loyal supporters (raving fans) and advocates for your brand. Moreover, don't overlook the importance of visual storytelling. Engaging visual content, such as captivating graphics and high-quality photography, can communicate your brand's story and values in an instant. Invest in professional branding assets that align with your brand's personality and allow them to tell your story visually.

Lastly, don't be afraid to evolve and adapt your content over time. As your business grows and changes, your brand identity may need to evolve with it. Stay attuned to your audience's needs and feedback and be open to making adjustments that better align with their desires and aspirations. Flexibility in evolving your content and brand identity is a mark of a strong, forward-thinking business. So, keep nurturing your content and brand with authenticity, consistency, emotional engagement, visual storytelling, and a spirit of adaptability. With each step you take on this business journey, remember that you are not alone. Lean into the supportive community of ambitious women, like the Eikonic Woman community, who are on a similar path of growth and success. Together, we can inspire one another and celebrate the collective achievements of empowered women. I'm excited to see how your brand identity continues to flourish!

It's time to Construct.

Now that you have a clear understanding of your target audience and the problem you'll be solving for them, it's time to construct your product or service in more detail.

Constructing your product or service in detail is crucial for several reasons. Firstly, it helps you align your offering with the specific needs and preferences of your target audience. By understanding your audience and the problem you are solving, you can design and develop a product or service that directly addresses their pain points. This targeted approach increases the chances of your offering gaining traction in the market and resonating with potential customers.

Secondly, constructing your product or service in more detail allows you to differentiate yourself from competitors. By clearly defining the core features, benefits, and scope of your offering, you can highlight what sets you apart and why customers should choose your product or service over others, (again highlighting the importance of your USP). This differentiation is vital in a crowded marketplace, as it helps you stand out and positions you as a preferred solution provider.

Additionally, a detailed construction gives you a solid foundation for pricing and packaging decisions. By understanding the value you are offering and the costs associated with its development and delivery, you can determine appropriate pricing levels that ensure profitability while remaining competitive. Furthermore, packaging options can be devised based on the varying needs and budgets of your target audience, allowing you to cater to different customer segments. Moreover, constructing your product or service in more detail enables you to test and iterate on your ideas. By creating prototypes, minimum viable products, or beta testing, you can gather feedback from a select group of users and make necessary improvements before launching to a wider audience. This iterative process helps you refine your offering, enhance its performance, and increase the chances of success in the market.

This whole process provides a solid foundation for your go-to-market strategy. With a clear understanding of your offering's unique features, benefits, and pricing, you can craft compelling marketing messages and develop targeted promotional materials. This ensures that your marketing efforts effectively communicate the value of your offering to your target audience, helping you attract customers and drive sales. When constructing their products or services, I get my clients to work through The Stress-free Productivity Process. This allows them to pay significant attention to three important elements such as Traffic, Tripwire, and Tail end.

Let me take a few minutes to break down each of these elements and their significance:

1. **Traffic**: Traffic refers to the number of people or potential customers who visit your website, store, or platform. It is crucial to attract a steady stream of relevant traffic to increase the chances of converting them into paying customers. To generate traffic, you can implement various strategies such as search engine optimisation (SEO), content marketing, social media advertising, influencer collaborations, and pay-per-click (PPC) advertising. The goal is to drive quality traffic to your product or service.

2. **Tripwire**: A tripwire is an irresistible and low-cost offer designed to convert traffic into customers. It acts as an entry point for customers to experience your product or service for the first time. The tripwire should provide enough value to entice customers but at a low price point. It serves as an opportunity to build trust and credibility, with the hope that

customers will be inclined to purchase additional products or services in the future. The tripwire offer should be carefully crafted to deliver value and exceed customer expectations.

3. **Tail End**: The tail end refers to the backend of your product or service offering, where you provide additional products, upsells, or high-value offerings to existing customers. It aims to maximise customer lifetime value and increase revenue. By analysing customer behaviour, preferences, and needs, you can identify opportunities to offer complementary products or services. Upselling, cross-selling, or offering exclusive upgrades can help you capitalise on existing customer relationships and increase their overall satisfaction with your brand.

Paying attention to these elements in your product or service construction can help you create a comprehensive and effective business model. By driving targeted traffic, providing an enticing tripwire offer, and leveraging the tail end, you can attract, convert, and retain customers, thus ensuring the growth and success of your business.

As a business owner, it's important to offer a variety of service levels to cater to clients with different needs and budgets. That's why it is essential to develop three levels of services to choose from if possible – 'Do It Yourself,' 'Do It With You,' and 'Do It For You' - so that your clients can select the level that best suits their needs.

'Do It Yourself' option is perfect for self-starters who like to take the reins on their own projects. With this level, you provide the resources, Tools and guidance necessary for clients to handle their own project independently. This is an economical option, as clients are responsible for most aspects of the project themselves.

This could take the shape of an online course and is more of a lower-end price product or service.

The "Do It With You" level is designed for clients who need some expert assistance but want to stay actively involved in the project. With this level, you/your team works together with the client at every step of the project, providing guidance, training, and support to achieve the desired outcome. This level is perfect for those who want to be involved but don't have the time or expertise to handle everything on their own. This could be a coaching programme, Masterclass, etc., and falls into the middle-tier pricing.

Finally, the "Do It For You" option is ideal for clients who need comprehensive, turnkey solutions and don't want to be burdened with the day-to-day aspects of the project. With this level, you/your team takes care of everything from design and implementation to execution and management. This option provides clients with complete peace of mind, knowing that they can trust you to deliver the desired result. This is more of a signature or premium-priced service.

Whichever level of service your clients choose, you have to be committed to providing them with the highest quality and most personalised service possible, ensuring that they are completely satisfied with the outcome of their results.

In summary, constructing your product or service in more detail is essential because it helps you align your offering with the needs of your target audience, differentiate yourself from competitors, make informed pricing and packaging decisions, iterate, and improve your ideas, and develop an effective go-to-market strategy. Taking the time to construct your offering in detail sets you up for success and increases the likelihood of delivering a valuable solution that resonates with your customers. Here's the thing, I completely understand how excitement and enthusiasm can lead to investing time and money into creating various coaching packages and products because I have been down that road. It's important to note that while passion is essential, conducting thorough market research and understanding your target audience's needs should always be the first step before investing resources.

Also, it is important to note that even though I say create, it is not about creating every single intricacy of the service you are creating but more about the outline. You want to start selling before you start going to that level of creation. Why? Because you do not want to spend all that time and money creating something that people end up not buying. So, sell and then start creating after you have had your first purchase – simple as.

Now, let us look at a few key points to help you avoid making some mistakes that I made – some points have been mentioned before, however, it is beneficial to reiterate so you recognise the importance:

1. **Market research**: Before creating new coaching packages or products, it's crucial to conduct thorough market research to understand your target audience's needs, pain points, and preferences. This will help you validate the demand for your offerings and ensure they align with what your audience is looking for.

    - **Define the benefits**: Clearly articulate the benefits your product or service offers to the customer. Think beyond the basic features and highlight the positive outcomes and transformations users can expect. Paint a picture of the positive impact your product or service can have on their lives.

2. **Target audience validation**: Always ensure that the target audience you are approaching is profitable. Consider factors such as their purchasing power and willingness to invest in coaching or products related to your niche. Understanding the financial viability of your target audience will help you avoid investing resources in areas that may not yield profitable returns.

  • **Consider packaging**: Take into account how you will package your product or service. Identify if there are any additional components, resources, tools, or materials that can enhance the overall value for your customers. Think about how you can make the experience more enjoyable and convenient for them.

  • **Decide on pricing**: Determine the pricing strategy for your product or service. Consider factors such as the perceived value, market competition, production costs, and the pricing expectations of your target audience. Strike a balance between profitability and affordability for your customers.

3. **Test and validate**: Instead of investing a significant amount of time and money upfront, consider starting with a minimal viable product or a smaller scale version of your coaching packages or products. Test these offerings with a select group of your target audience and gather feedback to validate whether it meets their needs and resonates with them. This iterative process allows you to refine and improve your offerings before scaling up.

  • **Identify the core features**: Note down the essential features that must be included in your product or service to effectively address your target audience's needs and solve their problem. These features should align with your value proposition and provide solutions in a unique and innovative way.

4. **Seek feedback**: Regularly seek feedback from your clients and customers to understand their experiences, satisfaction levels, and areas for improvement. This feedback loop will help you continuously refine and enhance your offerings based on their needs and preferences.

   • **Test and iterate**: Develop a prototype or create a small-scale version of your product or service to test it with a smaller group of users. Collect feedback, observe how people interact with it, and use that information to refine and iterate on your offering. This will help you improve the final product or service before its full launch.

5. **Measure success metrics**: Define success metrics for your coaching packages or products and regularly track and evaluate their performance. This will help you identify what's working and what's not, allowing you to make data-driven decisions in order to optimise for profitability and customer satisfaction.

   • **Determine the scope**: Decide the scope of your product or service. Will it be a single offering or a range of options? Consider how each option would cater to different segments of your target audience and offer various levels of value. This will help you provide options and cater to different price points.

6. **Open Shop!**: You need to promote and launch, unless your potential client knows that you exist well, they cannot buy, right? I will be speaking about this a bit further on in this chapter.

   - **Build your go-to-market plan**: As you finalise your product or service, it's important to create a comprehensive marketing and sales strategy. Determine the best channels and tactics to reach your target audience. Craft compelling messaging and create promotional materials that effectively communicate the value of your offering.
   - **Launch and refine**: With your product or service ready, it's time to launch it to the world. Keep an eye on user feedback and analytics to gauge its performance and identify areas for improvement. Continuously refine and enhance your offering based on customer insights and market trends.

By following these steps, you can ensure that the coaching packages or products you create are aligned with the needs of your target audience and have a higher chance of generating profit. Conducting thorough market research, validating your target audience's profitability, and testing your offerings before investing heavily will help you avoid the situation of having a beautiful shop with no traffic. Remember, understanding your customers' needs is essential to creating products or services that truly resonate and provide value in the market. Constructing a product or service requires careful planning, research, and iteration. Always keep your target audience's needs at the forefront and aim to deliver a product or service that exceeds their expectations. By continuously refining and improving your offering, you will be well-positioned for success in the marketplace.

Before I continue let me slip in a little bit about productisation – this strategy can help you grow your business and increase your revenue streams. Productisation is the process of turning your services or intangible products into valuable, marketable products that can be sold. By doing so, you can create a predictable revenue stream and increase your overall profitability. To productise your services, you can start by identifying your most popular and profitable offerings and then packaging them into a standardised format. This format could be a subscription model, a digital download, or a course. You can also consider adding complementary products or services to create a bundle that offers even more value to your customers.

When productising, it's important to ensure that your offerings deliver consistent value that meets your customers' needs and expectations. This means that you need to invest time in creating high-quality content, building a user-friendly platform, and providing excellent customer support. Remember, your customers' satisfaction is key to driving repeat purchases and positive word-of-mouth marketing.

Overall, it can be a valuable strategy for driving business growth and creating more predictable revenue streams. By creating valuable, marketable products that meet your customers' needs, you can increase your business's profitability and create a more sustainable future. Remember, building a product or service takes time and effort, but the reward of seeing your vision come to life is well worth it. As you embark on this exciting journey, stay true to your values and mission, continue to learn and adapt, and seek support from others who have gone through the process. And remember, if you need any further guidance throughout the process, the Eikonic Woman community is here to support you every step of the way.

Social media

https://qrco.de/bf6nvl

Go down the right *Channel*?

In this section I am speaking about Marketing channels. This plays a crucial role in getting your incredible product or service in front of the right audience. In today's competitive market, it's essential to stand out, and marketing channels provide the perfect avenue to showcase what you have to offer. A marketing channel refers to the different methods and platforms that businesses use to reach their target audience and promote their products or services. These channels serve as the pathways through which businesses communicate with their customers and distribute their offerings. By leveraging various marketing channels, you can ensure that your target customers find their way to your website or discover your product through different platforms. For example, social media platforms like Instagram offer the opportunity to reach potential customers as they casually scroll through their feeds. This way, you can capture the attention of those who may be desperately in need of what you're offering.

Marketing channels are not only about reaching new customers but also about keeping your existing customers engaged. By consistently using different channels to communicate with your audience, you can nurture the relationship and build loyalty. Moreover, utilising multiple marketing channels enables you to attract individuals from various backgrounds and walks of life. This broadens your customer base and helps create a powerful network that spreads the word about your product or service. Your passion and the value you bring deserve to be known and appreciated. By embracing and utilising different marketing channels with enthusiasm and strategic thinking, you can connect with your audience, share your story, and showcase the incredible value you offer. As you do so, you'll watch your dreams take flight, and your impact grow.

When thinking about how you are going to distribute your products or services, it is important to consider the following factors:

1. **Customer Communication**: You need to determine how you will communicate with your customers throughout the distribution process. This includes providing updates on order status, delivery notifications, and addressing any inquiries or concerns they may have. You can choose to handle customer communication in-house or outsource it to a customer service agency that specialises in managing customer inquiries.

2. **Sourcing**: You need to consider where you will source your products or materials from. This involves selecting suppliers or manufacturers that can reliably and efficiently produce or provide the items you need. You may choose to work with local suppliers, international suppliers, or a combination of both, depending on your specific requirements, cost considerations, and quality standards. Maybe for you it is not suppliers but instead hiring a powerhouse team to help you deliver the quality and experience that you want your clients to have.

3. **Technology**: Technology plays a vital role in modern distribution. You will need to determine the technological tools and systems that will support your distribution process effectively. This may include inventory management systems, order management systems, e-commerce platforms, logistics tracking software, and more. Investing in the right technology can streamline your operations, improve efficiency, and enhance the overall customer experience.

By carefully considering customer communication, sourcing strategies, and technology, you can optimise your distribution and fulfilment process. Remember to evaluate and adjust these factors periodically as your business grows and customer demands evolve. When selecting your marketing channels, it's important to consider your target audience, their preferences, and where they are most likely to engage with your brand. By choosing the right marketing channels, you can effectively reach your desired customers, build brand awareness, and drive sales. It's also crucial to regularly evaluate and adjust your marketing channel strategy to maximise results and stay ahead of the competition.

It's *Campaign* time!

A campaign is an essential component of a robust marketing strategy. It allows businesses to strategically plan and execute their marketing activities in a cohesive and targeted manner. By employing a variety of marketing channels, a campaign can effectively reach and engage with the target audience, maximising the impact of the promotional efforts. In a campaign, each marketing activity is carefully planned and coordinated to complement and reinforce the others. For example, advertisements can create initial awareness, content creation can provide more detailed information or showcase the product/service's benefits, social media engagement can foster interaction and build a community, and email marketing can nurture potential leads and convert them into customers.

So, when you are campaigning, it is not just about selling but also building a tribe. In any business, establishing long-term relationships, increasing customer loyalty, and driving growth is essential, and building client trust is the foundation for achieving these goals. To build and maintain trust with clients, several strategies need to be implemented. These strategies include consistent and transparent communication, delivering on promises, conducting business with integrity, providing exceptional customer service, showcasing expertise, prioritising confidentiality, seeking and acting on feedback, and fostering long-term relationships. By making trustworthiness part of your business culture and consistently acting on these strategies, you can foster trust leading to long-term success and growth.

Creating a Memorable Brand

Now let us take a look at a few steps my clients cover in the The Profitable T.R.I.B.E Builder, and as you can see the word T.R.I.B.E is an acronym so let's dig in.

Trust

Building client trust is a multifaceted and ongoing process that requires attention to detail and a commitment to excellence. Consistent communication is a cornerstone of trust-building. By keeping clients informed and involved at every stage of a project or transaction, you demonstrate transparency and reliability. Responding promptly to client inquiries and addressing their concerns shows that you value their input and are committed to their satisfaction.

Another crucial aspect of trust-building is delivering on promises. Consistently meeting or exceeding client expectations is vital for earning their trust. By delivering high-quality products or services and ensuring that deadlines are met, you demonstrate your reliability and dedication to their success. Should any issues arise, addressing them promptly and effectively is key to maintaining trust and showing your commitment to finding solutions.

Operating with integrity is essential in building and maintaining trust. Conducting business ethically and adhering to agreements and contracts reinforces trust. Honesty and transparency should be at the core of all interactions, even when mistakes are made. Taking responsibility for any errors and proactively working to rectify them goes a long way in maintaining trust and showing that you are accountable for your actions.

Exceptional customer service is another critical element in building trust. Going above and beyond to provide a positive and personalised experience for clients demonstrates your commitment to their satisfaction. Being responsive, attentive, and empathetic to their needs creates a sense of trust and reassurance that you value their business and are willing to go the extra mile.

Positioning yourself and your team as experts in your field is another trust-building strategy. Continuously investing in skill development, staying updated with industry trends, and sharing valuable insights with clients showcases your expertise. Clients are more likely to trust professionals who demonstrate a deep understanding of their needs and can provide effective solutions.

Respecting client confidentiality and privacy is paramount for building trust. Safeguarding their sensitive information and implementing robust data protection measures reassures clients that their information is secure. Adhering to relevant legal and industry standards and demonstrating your commitment to protecting client data further builds trust and confidence in your business. Also Seeking and acting on client feedback is invaluable in building trust. Encouraging clients to provide feedback on their experience working with you shows that you value their opinion and are committed to continuous improvement. Taking their input and suggestions seriously and actively working to address their concerns and incorporate their suggestions demonstrates your dedication to providing the best possible experience for your clients.

Focusing on fostering long-term relationships rather than solely pursuing short-term gains is vital. Demonstrating that you are invested in your clients' success and committed to supporting their long-term goals creates a sense of partnership and loyalty. Consistently providing value and nurturing the relationship beyond a single transaction deepens the trust and strengthens the bond between you and your clients. Remember, you don't just want a client; you want a raving fan.

Building client trust takes time, effort, and consistency. By prioritising trustworthiness in your business culture and values and actively implementing these strategies, you can establish and maintain the trust that leads to long-term success and growth. Trust is a valuable asset in any business relationship and contributes significantly to client satisfaction, loyalty, and business growth.

Relatability

Being relatable is essential because it allows you to connect with your target audience on a personal level. Consumers are more likely to engage with brands that they can relate to and resonate with. When you make your campaign or content relatable, it shows that you understand your audience's needs, challenges, and aspirations. By addressing their pain points and offering solutions that they can identify with, you build trust and credibility. Being relatable also humanises your brand, making it more approachable and trustworthy. When people feel a connection with your brand, they are more likely to develop loyalty and become advocates for your products or services. In a crowded marketplace, being relatable sets you apart from the competition and positions your brand as a trusted ally. It involves creating a sense of familiarity and common ground to build rapport and trust. There are various ways to be relatable in business.

Sharing your journey is an effective way to be relatable. By recounting relevant experiences and discussing challenges faced on your own journey and how you overcame them, customers can feel less isolated in their struggles and be inspired by your success. Additionally, showing vulnerability by being open and honest about limitations or mistakes humanises you and makes customers feel more comfortable and willing to engage with you. Actively listening is a key aspect of being relatable; it involves attentively and sincerely hearing customers' concerns or feedback without interruption or hasty conclusions. Demonstrating genuine interest and asking follow-up questions display your commitment to fully understanding their perspective. Furthermore, building a community provides opportunities for customers to connect with each other and share experiences. This fosters a sense of belonging and reinforces the idea that they are not alone in their journey. Remember, being relatable is about establishing authentic connections and trust. By demonstrating empathy, understanding, and openness, you can cultivate strong relationships with customers, leading to long-term loyalty and success in business.

Influence

As a business owner, embracing the role of an influencer can greatly benefit your brand. By following these tips, you can effectively connect with your target audience, showcase your expertise, and build credibility in your industry.

One of the key ways to assert yourself as an influencer is by sharing your knowledge and expertise. Utilise your platform to provide valuable insights, tips, strategies, and best practices that will assist your audience in resolving their challenges and achieving their goals. By positioning yourself as an expert, you will earn the trust and respect of your followers.

Authenticity and transparency are vital components of building trust with your audience. Share your journey, including both successes and failures. By being open about your processes, challenges, and lessons learnt, you make yourself relatable and forge a deeper connection with your audience. Your content should focus on providing value and solving problems for your audience. Identify their pain points and challenges and offer practical solutions that can help them overcome these obstacles. By consistently delivering valuable content, you position yourself as a go-to resource in your industry.

Engagement is key to building relationships with your audience. Take time to interact with them on social media, respond to comments and messages, and create opportunities for engagement. This level of interaction allows you to better understand your audience's needs and preferences, demonstrating that you genuinely care about their success.

Showcasing customer success stories can be a powerful way to build credibility and social proof. Highlight the outcomes and achievements of your customers or clients, showcasing the effectiveness of your products or services. Seeing real-life examples of others who have achieved positive results through your business will inspire trust and engagement among your audience.

Collaborating with other influencers in your industry can expand your reach and enhance your credibility. Partnering with reputable influencers allows you to tap into their audience and gain exposure to potential new customers or clients.

Remaining up-to-date with industry trends is essential. Stay informed about the latest news, developments, and advancements in your field. Share your insights and opinions on these topics to establish yourself as an industry thought leader. By staying current, you show your audience that you are knowledgeable and at the forefront of your industry.

Remember, as an influential business owner, your goal is to provide value, build trust, and establish yourself as a trustworthy source of information in your industry. By consistently delivering quality content and actively engaging with your audience, you can position yourself as a respected and influential figure in your field.

When you are working towards getting your business known, it is crucial to leverage influence because it allows you to effectively connect with your target audience, build trust, and drive desired actions. Influence helps you establish credibility and authenticity, making your brand more relatable and trustworthy in the eyes of your customers. By leveraging influencers, you can tap into their established audience and benefit from their reach, allowing you to expand your brand awareness and visibility. Influencers have the power to sway consumer opinions and purchasing decisions, making them valuable partners in amplifying your campaign's message. Additionally, influencers often have specialised knowledge and expertise in their respective fields, enabling them to authentically endorse your brand or product. By strategically incorporating influence into your campaign, you can enhance your brand's reputation, drive engagement, and ultimately achieve your business goals.

Brand

The relevance of your brand is of utmost importance when campaigning as it directly impacts the effectiveness and success of your efforts. A relevant brand is one that aligns seamlessly with the needs, interests, and values of your target audience. When your brand is relevant, it demonstrates an understanding of your audience's challenges and desires, allowing you to create messaging that resonates with them on a deeper level. One of the main reasons why brand relevance is important in a campaign is that it establishes a strong connection with your audience. When people feel that your brand understands and relates to their specific needs and aspirations, they are more likely to pay attention to your messages and engage with your campaign. Relevance makes your brand relatable, and relatability builds trust.

A relevant brand campaign goes beyond generic marketing tactics and focuses on addressing the specific pain points and challenges that your target audience faces. By highlighting how your products or services can solve these problems, you position your brand as a relevant solution provider. This approach not only captures the attention of your audience but also encourages them to take action and choose your brand over competitors.

Ultimately, the relevance of your brand in a campaign creates a sense of affinity and connection with your audience, increasing the likelihood of engagement, loyalty, and advocacy. By tailoring your messages to meet your clients unique needs, you establish a competitive edge and position your brand as a trusted and relevant choice in the minds of consumers.

Engagement

Engaging with clients during a campaign is not only important but also necessary for its success. It serves as a means to build strong relationships, foster customer loyalty, and drive meaningful interactions. When you engage with clients during a campaign, you establish a sense of trust and credibility. Engagement with clients also provides an opportunity for two-way communication. It allows you to convey important campaign messages, while also enabling your clients to provide their thoughts, opinions, and suggestions. This exchange of information can offer valuable insights into their expectations, preferences, and pain points, which can inform future campaign strategies and enhance the overall effectiveness of your efforts.

There are several ways to engage with clients during a campaign. One effective method is through social media platforms, where you can actively listen and respond to comments, messages, and mentions. This not only shows your commitment to excellent customer service but also enables you to have real-time conversations with your clients. You can also utilise surveys, polls, and questionnaires to gather more targeted feedback and insights. By involving clients in decision-making processes, such as voting for campaign elements or seeking their opinions on product development, you make them feel valued and connected to your brand.

Furthermore, hosting events, webinars, or live streams provides a platform for direct interaction with clients. These engagements can include Q&A sessions, demonstrations, or informative discussions related to your campaign objectives. This face-to-face or virtual interaction allows for a deeper understanding of client perspectives and enables you to provide personalized responses to their inquiries or concerns.

Overall, client engagement during a campaign is essential as it fosters a sense of connection, loyalty, and mutual understanding. By actively involving clients in conversations and seeking their input, you establish strong relationships and create a foundation for long-term success. Engaging with clients not only improves your campaign's impact, but it also helps you refine your strategies, deliver better customer experiences, and drive the continued growth and success of your business.

Finally, there are several ways to run a business campaign depending on your goals, target audience, and resources. Here are some common approaches:

1. **Digital Marketing**: Utilise online channels, such as search engines, social media, email marketing, and display advertising, to promote your business and reach a wide audience. Create compelling content, optimise your website for search engines, and leverage social media platforms to engage with your target audience.

2. **Content Marketing**: Develop and distribute valuable and relevant content, such as blog posts, videos, infographics, and eBooks. This approach aims to attract and engage your target audience by providing them with useful information and building brand authority.

3. **Social Media Campaigns**: Focus on leveraging social media platforms to reach and engage with your target audience. Develop engaging campaigns, contests, or challenges to foster interactions and encourage user-generated content. Utilise paid advertising on social media platforms to increase visibility and reach.

4. **Influencer Marketing**: Collaborate with influencers or individuals who have a strong following and influence in your target market. They can promote your products or services to their audience, generating interest and trust in your brand.

5. **Email Marketing**: Build and maintain an email list of interested customers or prospects. Send targeted and personalised emails to promote your campaign, share updates, and offer exclusive deals or content.

6. **Search Engine Advertising**: Run paid search engine advertising campaigns to display ads on search engine results pages. This allows you to target specific keywords and reach potential customers who are actively searching for products or services similar to yours.

7. **Offline Advertising**: Consider traditional advertising methods such as TV, radio, print media, billboards, or direct mail if they align with your target audience and campaign goals. These mediums can be effective for reaching local or specific demographic segments.

8. **Partnership or Affiliate Marketing**: Collaborate with other businesses or influential individuals in your industry to promote your products or services. This can include cross-promotion, affiliate marketing programs, or joint campaigns that benefit both parties.

9. **Event Marketing**: Organise or participate in events, trade shows, or conferences relevant to your industry. This provides opportunities to showcase your brand, network with potential customers, and generate leads.

10. **Referral Programs**: Develop referral programs to incentivize your current customers to refer new customers to your business. Word-of-mouth marketing can be highly effective in generating trust and attracting new customers.

11. **Public Relations**: Use public relations strategies to generate media coverage, positive press, or thought leadership opportunities. This can enhance your brand reputation and increase visibility to a wider audience.

Remember to set clear campaign objectives, define your target audience, and track and measure your results. Choosing the right combination of campaign methods and channels will depend on your business's resources, target audience, and specific goals. Regular analysis and optimisation will help you refine your campaign strategies and maximise your return on investment.

Running a campaign is indeed about making your presence known and showcasing what you have to offer. It's about grabbing your potential clients' attention, creating interest, and ultimately enticing them to engage with your business.

Unlike what many tend to think, running a campaign is an ongoing process that requires consistent effort and the willingness to adapt. It's crucial to maintain a strong presence and continuously refine your approach. By monitoring, learning, and adjusting based on your target audience's feedback, you'll be able to effectively attract and engage potential clients. Given the complexities involved, it can be beneficial to outsource certain aspects of your campaign. Focus on what you're skilled at and passionate about, and delegate tasks that you're less comfortable with. By leveraging the expertise of others, you can optimise your strengths and make the most of your campaign efforts. Planning, hard work, and strategic outsourcing can greatly enhance your chances of success.

- *The Power of Storytelling*
- *Pen to Profits*
- *Get on Stage*

Utilising
The Power
of Your Story

CHAPTER FOUR

Utilising The Power of Your Story

"When you realise that your story is actually not yours and instead is a gift to the world, you can no longer keep it to yourself."

MICHELLE WATSON

The Power of Storytelling

Let's dive into the exciting world of storytelling, imagine this scenario: You're on a website that features a range of organic skincare products. Each product appears to be similar, with similar features and claims. How do you decide which one to purchase?

Now, picture finding a product with a unique selling point: storytelling. The product's founder shares a heartwarming story about her daughter's lifelong struggle with acne and how she discovered a natural ingredient that changed her life. The founder goes on to discuss how her success inspired her to start her own brand. Compared to the other products, which one would you choose to buy?

Most likely, you'd choose the product with a story. That's because storytelling has the ability to capture our attention, resonate with our emotions, and persuade us to take action.

Storytelling isn't just a marketing gimmick. It's a critical skill for entrepreneurs, business owners, and leaders who want to stand out in today's crowded and competitive marketplace. In this chapter, you'll discover a bit more about storytelling, how it can benefit your business, and how to master this essential skill. I shared my story at the beginning of this book as it gave you an insight into my journey. You may have found bits that you resonated with, found inspiring, or that encouraged you. This is the same that happens to your audience when you share your story. And please, do not say you do not have a story. We all do – the journey and destination may be different, but every story is unique and there will always be someone out there waiting to hear yours so that they too can be encouraged. There are people that would resonate with your story more than mine – so do keep that in mind. No story is too small.

What exactly is storytelling, and why does it hold such importance?

At its core, storytelling is the art of creating narratives that capture the essence of your brand and resonate with your audience. It involves crafting messages that are relatable, memorable, and go beyond the mere features and benefits of your product or service. Throughout my extensive experience as an entrepreneur, speaker, author, and mentor, I've discovered that storytelling delves into the emotional and psychological aspects of your audience's decision-making process.

While storytelling is not a new concept and has been prevalent in various cultural histories, its application extends beyond education and entertainment. It plays a significant role in the business world as well. Some of the most successful brands and leaders, such as Apple, Nike, Elon Musk, Martin Luther King Jr., and Oprah, have harnessed the power of storytelling in their sales, marketing, and leadership. What binds them together is the presence of a compelling narrative.

Let us explore the benefits of storytelling, which I've observed both within the business sector and in my personal experience.

These benefits can be summarised into five key points:

1. Building Trust and Rapport with Your Audience

    In business, establishing a connection with your audience is crucial. People tend to buy from brands they like, trust, and feel familiar with. By incorporating storytelling into your brand strategy, you can showcase your personality, values, and authenticity. This helps to build trust, fostering a likable and relatable image that resonates with customers.

2. Differentiating Your Brand from Competitors

    In a competitive marketplace, it's essential to stand out and demonstrate your unique selling proposition. Storytelling offers a powerful tool for highlighting what sets you apart from others in your industry. By crafting and sharing the right narrative, you can effectively communicate what makes your brand special and better. Your story becomes a compelling reason for customers to choose you.

3. Creating Memorable and Shareable Content

    Think back to seminars or talks you've attended where the speakers have shared stories about renowned figures like Elon Musk or Mark Zuckerberg. These stories tend to remain memorable despite the constant influx of information we encounter daily. Stories cut through the noise, capturing attention, and leaving a lasting impression. By leveraging storytelling in your content, you can make your message memorable, easily recalled, and highly shareable, leading to increased brand exposure.

4. Increasing Loyalty and Engagement

   To maintain an engaged audience, it's essential to offer an emotional experience. Your audience should feel a connection and spark when interacting with your brand. This is where storytelling excels. Stories have the power to evoke emotions, making your audience care deeply about your message. By incorporating well-crafted narratives, you can enhance user engagement, promote customer retention, and foster brand loyalty.

5. Driving Sales and Conversions

   Sometimes, decisions are driven by emotions and then justified with logic. Stories have the ability to influence emotions, motivating people to act. They can address objections and fears while creating a sense of urgency and scarcity. By implementing storytelling techniques, you can tap into the emotional aspect of decision-making, ultimately driving sales and increasing conversion rates.

In summary, embracing storytelling in your business strategy can help you build trust, differentiate your brand, create memorable content, increase engagement, and drive sales. Incorporating compelling narratives is a powerful way to connect with your audience, leaving a long-lasting impact on their perception of your brand.

There are various ways you can share your unique story with the world, so let us take a moment to explore some of them:

1. **Social Media Platforms**: In this digital age, social media platforms like Instagram, Facebook, Twitter, and LinkedIn offer fantastic opportunities to share your story. Through captivating posts, videos, and even live streams, you can connect with your audience and share your journey, values, and triumphs. Embrace the power of storytelling on these platforms to reach a wider audience and spark meaningful conversations.

2. **Blogging and Content Creation**: If you have longer-form thoughts and insights to share, blogging is a wonderful platform to unleash your storytelling prowess. Create a blog or contribute to existing platforms where you can write articles, share personal experiences, and impart valuable advice. By offering a deep and thought-provoking narrative, you can build a loyal community and establish yourself as an authority in your field.

3. **Public Speaking and Presentations**: Don't underestimate the impact of public speaking in sharing your story – I love it! Whether it's through conferences, webinars, panels, or workshops, speaking engagements provide a live and immersive experience for your audience. Take the stage with confidence, speak from the heart, and let your story inspire and empower those who listen.

4. **Podcasts and Interviews**: The rise of podcasts has opened up another avenue for sharing your story. Consider hosting your own podcast or being a guest on established shows. Engage in heartfelt conversations, exchange insights, and connect with podcast audiences who are eager to learn from your journey. Remember, the power of your voice can resonate deeply with listeners around the world.

5. **Collaborations and Partnerships**: Joining forces and collaborating with like-minded individuals and brands can extend the reach of your story even further. Seek out opportunities for partnerships, guest posts, and cross-promotions. By aligning your brand with others that share similar values, you can amplify your story and collectively uplift each other.

6. **Become an Author**: Just picture the endless possibilities of using a book to share your incredible story – a story that will leave a lasting legacy, inspire generations, and ignite a transformative spark in the hearts of readers across the globe. Embracing the enchanting power of storytelling through a book is a truly remarkable way to share your journey, insights, and the invaluable lessons that have shaped you. By wholeheartedly embracing the power of a book, you can illuminate the lives of countless others in a profoundly impactful way. Your voice, your experiences – they matter. They have the power to inspire, motivate, and uplift others on their own journeys. So, pick up that pen or laptop, let your creativity flow, and create a masterpiece that will touch the hearts and minds of readers for generations to come. This is how my journey started, so I have no doubt that it works.

Now, let me share with you some tips on how to tap into the magical force of storytelling.

Embrace the Journey: Whether writing a book or getting on stage to share your story, it is an invitation to dive deep into your personal experiences - to reflect on the highs, lows, and life-changing lessons that have defined you. It's an opportunity to embrace your unique journey, letting your authenticity shine through, and an avenue to get your audience to resonate with you. It's an open door for you to position yourself as an expert. For this reason, it is time for you to courageously share your vulnerable moments. Through your resilience and growth, you will be able to inspire others to find their own path to greatness.

Craft a Compelling Narrative: Think of your platform as a canvas for the remarkable art of storytelling. Weave together a narrative that captures the audience's heart, taking them on an emotional rollercoaster as they traverse the valleys and celebrate the peaks of your struggles, triumphs, and victories. Infuse your warmth into every word, painting vivid images that transport them into your world, leaving an indelible impression on their souls. Share with them the problems you experienced; this should tap into their needs and pains.

Offer Practical Wisdom: As you share your story, remember to include practical wisdom – tangible advice, actionable steps, and empowering insights that readers can apply to their own lives. Empower them to overcome their obstacles, helping them unlock their truest potential. Your words are like gentle steppingstones guiding them on their unique journey of growth and self-discovery. This is where the catalyst moment happens; they want to know what transformation took place and how. They want to know how you have managed to get from point A, where they are currently, to point B, where you are now and where they desire to be. In essence, your story should address some of your clients NDP's (N' needs, desires, and pain points. Create a Sense of Community: A story holds the remarkable power to create a sense of belonging and connectedness. Share personal anecdotes and relatable experiences, allowing your readers to feel seen, heard, and truly understood. Invite them to join you on a transformative journey, fostering collective empowerment and celebrating shared success. Together, we are stronger.

Elevate Empathy and Understanding: Stories possess a truly magical ability to bridge gaps, cultivating empathy and understanding across diverse backgrounds and cultures. Your story has the power to transcend societal boundaries, encouraging deeper connections and a greater appreciation for our shared humanity. By sharing your unique perspective and illuminating universal truths, you cultivate a sense of unity and interconnectedness that is so desperately needed in our world.

I want to take a closer look at the two platforms I successfully used to get my story out there and helped set me on the path of entrepreneurship.

Pen to Profits

Have you ever thought about writing a book? Have you had life experiences that taught you important lessons that you want to share with others? Writing a self-help book or a book of lessons about life drawn from your own experiences is a powerful tool to use for marketing your business and positioning you as an expert in your field. I understand that getting started and turning your story and content into a book can be a bit overwhelming, but it is a beautiful and powerful way of not only getting your story and content in front of your potential audience but also you have the chance to leave a legacy behind.

I've had the pleasure of working with many authors who have weaved their personal stories into self-help books. So, to kickstart your journey or help you get unstuck, let me share some ideas on how you can begin turning your story into a book.

First, start with the most important story. Choose the story that you feel is the most impactful and meaningful to your journey and your target audience. If you could only tell three stories from your life, what would they be? If you already use anecdotes to illustrate points in your work or when communicating with others, what are the top three stories you like to share that relates to your audience or showcases your brand story? Begin by getting these key stories onto the page. When writing your story, embrace your own voice. The voice you use when telling your story to someone else may not be the exact voice you use in your final draft. However, it's important to capture your true essence and style. Try telling your stories on paper or by dictating them into software that transcribes your words. You can even record yourself telling your story and use transcription services to convert them into written words.

To truly engage your readers, put them in the moment. Instead of simply narrating, telling them about an event or experience, show them. Use sensory details to bring your story to life - the sounds, sights, smells, and feelings. Make the moment come alive in the mind of your reader. They need to be able to create the image in their mind as they read. Don't be afraid to infuse humour, too, especially when recounting moments where you stumbled or made a funny mistake. When you're starting out, don't worry too much about the writing itself. Great storytellers don't always rely on fancy language. Remember, this is just the beginning, and your inner critic should take a backseat for now. Let your stories flow freely without overthinking or editing prematurely. You can refine and polish your writing later. One of the most powerful ways to connect with readers is by being emotionally honest about your experiences. Emotional experiences are what deeply connect us as humans. If you've been through something others haven't, they'll be naturally curious and want to experience it vicariously through your story. Allow yourself to be open and vulnerable, paint the emotional scenes. Describe your reactions, the way you coped, how you felt, and the impact it had on your life. Let yourself be vulnerable on the page because that's what makes you relatable and creates a genuine connection with readers. Remember, you are the storyteller, and your story should be told in your unique way. There is no right or wrong way to share your experiences. Embrace your truth and tell your story from your perspective. Don't worry about other people's versions of events at this stage. Start with what is true to you and your memories.

If you truly want your story of suffering or struggle to inspire others, it's essential to let them experience that transformative moment, that catalytic moment when everything changed for you. Whether it was finding your voice, walking away from a toxic situation, or stepping bravely into the unknown, that powerful moment needs to be felt by your readers. It's that surge of triumph that will pull them in, leaving them hungry to learn more about your experiences and the wisdom you've gained along the way. When you open up and share those pivotal moments, you create a deep connection with your readers. They want to witness your transformation, to feel the same surge of empowerment that propelled you forward. By allowing them to experience the triumph, you ignite their own inner spark and kindle a desire for personal growth and change. Don't hold back. Let them feel the adrenaline, the joy, and the hope that came forth from your journey. Show them the power of resilience, determination, and the strength that lies within each of us. Your story has the ability to inspire countless others who may be on their own path of struggle or in need of a source of hope. Remember, by sharing your triumph, you invite others to explore the possibilities that await them. You become a guiding light, showing the way and reminding them of their own potential for greatness. So, go ahead and infuse your writing with that empowering energy. Let your story ignite a fire within readers, urging them to embark on their own transformative journey. Writing a book that serves as a marketing tool allows you to authentically connect with your audience on a deeper level. Rather than simply promoting your products or services, you have the opportunity to create a genuine connection by sharing the journey that led you to where you are today. Your book becomes a powerful avenue for not only showcasing your expertise but also establishing yourself as a trusted authority within your field. When readers see the transformation you've experienced, the lessons you've learned, and the success you've achieved, they can't help but be inspired to join you on your journey.

With your book as a marketing tool, you have the opportunity to reach a wider audience, amplify your message, and attract those who align with your purpose and values. It becomes a beautiful bridge that connects you with like-minded individuals, fostering a sense of community and shared growth.

You also want to share your content in the book by addressing the pain points and the solution you provide. You may be thinking, "Michelle, that is too much information," but you need to understand that you must give them enough to see you as an expert but also leave them incomplete so that they want to hear more. The next thing is that you are giving the what and not the how. As one of my mentors, Andy Harrington, says, *"information for free and implementation for a fee."* For instance, if you are a coach, let your chapters take the shape of your modules, and your subtitles become the various steps each module covers.

So, as you embark on this exciting venture of writing your book and using it as a marketing tool, remember that your authenticity and genuine desire to empower others will be the foundation of your success.

Use your words to inspire, uplift, and connect - because when we uplift one another, we all rise together.

Get on Stage

As a speaker, sharing your story is a powerful way to connect with your audience on a deep and personal level. It's a chance to inspire, motivate, and uplift others by offering them a glimpse into your own journey of growth, resilience, and triumph. Your story has the potential to create a profound impact, leaving a lasting impression on those who have the privilege of hearing it. When you step onto that stage and open up about your experiences, you give permission for others to do the same. You create a safe space for vulnerability, allowing your audience to reflect on their own lives and find the courage to face their own challenges. I had the experience of speaking at an event and it gave a woman in her twenties the opportunity to come to me after the talk and reveal that her father had molested her when she was a child. At that time, she had still not told anyone, not even her mother. I have had more than one of these types of scenarios, and having these experiences has made me bolder and more open to speak and share from a vulnerable place. By sharing your story, you become a beacon of hope, showing others that they are not alone and that transformation is possible.

One of the greatest strengths of sharing your story as a speaker is the ability to inspire authentic connection. Your audience is not just listening to another motivational speech; they are hearing your truth, your struggles, and your triumphs. Through your words, they witness firsthand the power of resilience, determination, and personal growth. In turn, they feel seen, heard, and understood, igniting a sense of shared experience and collective growth.

When crafting your speaking engagement, remember to infuse your story with emotion. Share the highs and lows, the moments of doubt, and the moments of triumph. Your vulnerability will resonate deeply with your audience, allowing them to empathise with your journey and feel inspired to overcome their own obstacles. By being authentic and genuine, you create a connection that goes beyond mere words. I have realised on my journey as a speaker that your story is not just about you; it's about the impact you can make on the lives of your audience. Every word you speak has the potential to spark a transformation within someone's heart and mind. By sharing your story, you have the power to inspire change, motivate action, and empower others to believe in their own potential.

> *When we uplift one another,*
> *we all rise together.*

So, don't be afraid to share your story as a speaker. Embrace the opportunity to connect with your audience, to make a difference, and to create a ripple effect of positive change. Your voice matters, and your story has the potential to touch countless lives.

Do not wait to be a polished speaker before you start sharing. I started out by sharing my testimony in church, then sharing in small women's groups, and doing live streams on Facebook. I never thought of it as speaking, but just sharing. That sharing eventually led me to big stages. My point is you must start somewhere; it could be in your church, your workplace, or even on your social media platform.

You will never know where it could lead you until you embark on the journey. The beauty of transforming lives by sharing your story as a speaker is remarkable. With your empowering words and genuine connection, you can inspire and uplift others in ways you may never have imagined. Keep shining your light and creating a ripple of positive impact. I can't wait to hear about your experience of starting your speaking journey and speaking engagements to transform the lives of those who have the privilege of hearing your story.

Remember, your story is unique, powerful, and worthy of being shared. Embrace the various platforms available to you and ensure that your voice is heard far and wide. The world is waiting to be inspired by your journey, values, and triumphs. "*A story not shared, is a message not heard and a life not saved.*"

> **A story not shared, is a message not heard and a life not saved.**

Watch me

https://qrco.de/bf6oJO

- *Mindset*
- *Money*
- *Mastery*
- *Momentum*

Creating
Balance
Success in All Areas
of Your Life

CHAPTER FIVE

Creating Balance

Success in All Areas of Your Life

"There is a price to pay for success, there is also a price to pay for failure. The question is, what price are you willing to pay?"

FELA BANK-OLEMOH

As a woman, you have incredible potential to create success in all areas of your life - whether it's in your career, relationships, personal development, or overall well-being. You have the power within you to achieve greatness. To create success, start by defining what success means to you. What are your personal aspirations? What do you value most in life? Understanding your own definition of success is crucial in determining the path you want to take. I've had many clients who come to me stating that what they desire is success or wealth. My first question to them is, what does that look like?

Success and wealth are subjective concepts that can look different to each individual. What defines success or wealth for one person may not be the same for another. Personally, I wanted to create my desired life right from the beginning. In order to do that, I needed to know what that looked like. I would do exercises like the "perfect day exercise" and create my "magic number". I created an image of how my forties would look like, as this would help determine what my life would look like when I reached fifty. I took the initiative to determine what my desired life would look like doing these exercises. These exercises can be very helpful in visualising the life you want to create for yourself.

I made notes about what that looked like, and here's a summary of the key aspects I identified:

1. **Ideal yearly income**: I determined the figure that would allow me to live comfortably and achieve financial stability.

2. **Time freedom and how I wanted to spend it**: I recognised the importance of having both time and money freedom. Because I value having control over my schedule and being able to spend my time in ways that align with my priorities and interests.

3. **My Marriage**: Being able to enjoy life with my husband and create a foundation together where we leave an inheritance and legacy for our lineage. This includes setting an example of a healthy, loving relationship.

4. **Independence and entrepreneurship**: I expressed the desire to not work for anyone before the age of fifty and to run my own business. This indicated my preference for being my own boss, having autonomy in decision-making, and being able to choose who I worked with, where I worked, and how I worked.

5. **Alignment with spiritual beliefs**: The aspiration to be free to follow the direction of God without constraints. Because I value having the freedom to align my work and life choices with my personal spiritual beliefs and being able to give back.

6. **Quality family experiences**: Being able to spend quality time and being able to afford special experiences with my family was of vital importance.

By having a clear vision and understanding of what success and prosperity means to you, you have established a foundation for creating a life that aligns with your aspirations. It's important to remember that your definition of success and riches is unique to you, and it may evolve over time. Using your identified priorities and goals, you can develop strategies and take actionable steps to work towards the life you desire. It's important to acknowledge and respect the diversity of perspectives and definitions when it comes to these concepts. Each person has unique goals, values, and aspirations that shape their own understanding of success or riches. Some may prioritise financial abundance and material possessions, while others may focus on personal growth, meaningful relationships, or making a positive impact in the world. Success and wealth can also be measured by factors such as happiness, fulfilment, health, or balance in different areas of life. It's crucial to consider your own aspirations and definition of success when pursuing your goals. By understanding your personal desires and values and tailoring strategies and support accordingly, you can create a path towards your version of success and riches.

One thing you may notice is that I did not have health on my list, as at the time, it was not of importance to me. Let me keep it real—I was on the hustle vibe, and self-care went out the window. This is a common mistake many of us make. As I stated earlier, we enter the avenue of building our life around the business instead of the business around our life. We get so consumed and lose balance as the hustle gets all the focus. I made this important observation when a health issue arose, and not including health on my list of priorities at the time slowly began to change, and it became a priority as I then had no choice. It is a common mistake that many people make, especially when they are in a hustle mindset like I was and focused solely on building the business or pursuing the goals. In the pursuit of success, self-care and maintaining a healthy balance often gets the backseat.

It's important to recognise the significance of health as a foundational element of overall well-being and long-term success. Neglecting self-care and sacrificing balance can have negative consequences on various aspects of life, including physical and mental health, relationships, and overall happiness. Building a life that revolves solely around business or career aspirations may lead to burnout, deteriorating health, and strained relationships. It is crucial to remember that success should not come at the expense of your well-being and personal fulfilment. What is the point of having the money but not being around to enjoy it. Finding a balance between personal and professional aspects of life is key. Prioritising self-care, including physical activity, proper nutrition, and mental well-being, can contribute to increased energy, focus, and overall productivity. Taking breaks, establishing boundaries, and engaging in activities that bring joy and relaxation are also essential for maintaining a healthy work-life balance. Remember, building a fulfilling and successful life involves integrating your personal desires and values into your professional endeavours. By prioritising health and ensuring a harmonious balance between work and personal life, you can cultivate long-term success and well-being. I struggled with self-care for a long time because it felt to me like selfish-care. I have always been a people person, always putting others first until I realised that I cannot pour from an empty cup. There is a reason why when on a flight the air hostess instructs us to put our oxygen mask on first before doing so for others – think about it, how many people can YOU help when you are dead? How many lives can you save if yours is prematurely cut off because you didn't take the time to love and nurture yourself first?

It's important to prioritise self-care and personal development. Take care of your physical, mental, and emotional well-being. Dedicate time each day to activities that bring you joy, reduce stress, and help you grow as an individual. This could include exercise, meditation, reading, or engaging in hobbies that ignite your passion. Have a support network of like-minded individuals. Surround yourself with positive and inspiring people who believe in your potential and will encourage your growth. Seek out mentors and role models who can provide guidance and support along your journey.

Embrace a growth mindset; we will speak some more about this soon. View challenges as opportunities for growth and learning. Do not let setbacks deter you from pursuing your goals. Instead, learn from them and use them as steppingstones towards future success. Find a healthy work-life balance that allows you to excel in your hustle while also nurturing your personal life. Learn to set boundaries and prioritise your time wisely. Remember that success is not solely measured by professional achievements but also by the happiness and fulfilment you experience in your personal life.

I believe that having a balanced life as a woman is where the true success lies. Having a balanced life means that a woman is able to effectively juggle and prioritise different aspects of her life in a way that nurtures her well-being and allows her to thrive in all areas. It means finding harmony and fulfillment in various roles and responsibilities, whether it be in your career, business, relationships, family, personal growth, or self-care. A balanced life as a woman involves setting boundaries, managing time wisely, and making intentional choices that aligns with your values and priorities. It means recognising the importance of self-care and ensuring we take care of our physical, emotional, and mental health. A balanced life empowers us to live authentically, pursue our purpose, and maintain healthy relationships. Ultimately, a balanced life enables you to lead a fulfilling, purpose-driven, and successful life that embraces all aspects of who you are.

Now I am going to share a few M's that I normally work with my Eikonic Women through in 'The Wealthy Women Principles Module.'

Embracing a Successful *Mindset*

In this section, we dive deep into the concept of mindset, which I firmly believe is the most crucial element in overcoming any challenge life throws your way and in having success. We spoke briefly about having a growth mindset earlier, but mindset is one that we really have to elaborate on.

A successful mindset is a way of thinking that empowers individuals to achieve their goals and create the life they desire. It involves adopting a positive, growth-oriented outlook, setting clear goals, believing in oneself, approaching challenges with resilience, and continuously learning and growing. A successful mindset enables you to stay focused on your desired outcomes and take consistent action towards them, even when obstacles arise. It involves cultivating supportive beliefs and habits that enhance confidence, motivation, and productivity. By embracing a successful mindset, you can unleash your full potential, overcome limitations, and achieve long-term success and fulfilment.

> *True transformation begins within your mind.*

Without correcting your mindset, any steps you take towards personal growth and improvement will ultimately fall short. Attending seminars and workshops can be inspiring and motivating, but true transformation begins within your mind. It's not about suddenly becoming a completely different person overnight, but rather the gradual process of lifting yourself from the depths to the heights you can reach. I can vividly recall my own personal prison, trapped within a mindset that kept me unaware of my true potential. It was only when I confronted and corrected my mindset that I was able to break free and begin building the life I desired. Until you recognise where you may be going wrong, it's easy to believe that you are content and living a fulfilling life. However, settling for mediocrity is not the path to true happiness. I had to change my mindset not just for myself, but also to guide and support others and to tap into my full potential. I chose to move away from the limiting beliefs that many people in the world accept about their challenges. I mentioned this verse before, Romans 12:2, about not conforming to the ways of the world but rather being transformed by the renewing of our minds. Transformation requires continually renewing your mind, clearing out the negative clutter that the world tries to feed you and undermine your progress. When our mindset is influenced by what everyone else around us is doing, it will only yield the same results that everyone else is experiencing. To ensure positive outcomes, we must deliberately feed our minds with the right information. One practice I've incorporated into my routine is to start each day with my morning devotion (prayer, reading my Bible (the truth), worship, and meditation). I listen to audiobooks, podcasts, as well as great speakers and sermons. By intentionally feeding my mind with positivity during the first few hours of the day, I set the tone for a productive and empowering day ahead and equips me to handle the challenges that may arise ahead.

> *However, settling for mediocrity is not the path to true happiness.*

I also encourage you to challenge yourself to read or listen to at least one book per month. Books have the power to expand our minds, challenge our perspectives, and inspire change. Whether you choose personal development books, biographies, or fiction that resonates with your soul, reading opens a world of knowledge and fresh insights. Remember, your mindset is the foundation upon which your entire life is built. Take the time to assess your beliefs, challenge your self-imposed limitations, and intentionally create a mindset that propels you towards growth and success. I invite you to reflect on the power of a transformed mindset. Embrace the journey of renewing your mind daily and witness the incredible impact it has on your personal growth and the fulfilment of your potential. Your mind is the powerhouse that drives your life, and the inputs you provide determine the outputs you receive. To become the person you aspire to be, it is crucial to program your mind for success. Envision yourself already accomplishing your goals and let your mind embrace that vision. By doing so, you are setting your course towards achieving what you desire. Remember, with God nothing is impossible. Once you program your mind to believe in something, and your desires are in alignment with God's will, you can achieve it.

What is it that you want to accomplish?

What challenges are you currently facing that may seem insurmountable due to your environment and circumstances?

I urge you to, as you read this book, program your mind to see your success. Surround yourself with positive thoughts and people, whilst feeding your mind with uplifting and empowering messages. Remember that what you put in is what you will get back out, so if you are feeding your brain rubbish, do not expect the golden nuggets. Additionally, seek out the company of successful individuals who can inspire and motivate you on your journey. It is time for you to tap into that greatness within you and maximise your full potential. Take those challenges you are facing and transform them into opportunities for personal growth and renewal. By consciously shaping your mindset, you have the power to overcome any obstacles that may come your way. Embrace the process of rewiring your mind and watch as it propels your life towards your version of success.

> *Your mind is the powerhouse that drives your life, and the inputs you provide determine the outputs you receive.*

Money - Financial Freedom is bliss

Becoming financially free as a woman is a powerful journey towards independence and empowerment. It involves taking control of one's financial situation, making informed decisions, and building wealth for a secure future. This journey starts with understanding and valuing one's financial worth and capabilities. By prioritising financial literacy and education, you can equip yourself with the knowledge and skills necessary to make sound financial choices. This includes budgeting, saving, investing, and managing debt effectively. In addition, fostering a mindset of abundance and believing in one's ability to create wealth is essential. Breaking through societal norms and overcoming gender biases, you can forge your own path to financial freedom. By building a strong financial foundation, you can experience the freedom to pursue your passions, contribute to your communities, and achieve your dreams.

> *If you are feeding your brain rubbish, do not expect the golden nuggets.*

Prioritising financial independence and building a diversified income portfolio is crucial for us as women. This involves exploring various income streams such as entrepreneurship, investments, and passive income sources. By diversifying your income, you not only enhance your financial stability but also gain the flexibility to pursue your passions and create the life you envision. As my nan always reminded me growing up, it is wise to "never put all your eggs in one basket." By diversifying and splitting your resources into separate baskets, you can mitigate risks. If one basket were to drop, you still have the eggs from the other basket to rely on. Similarly, by diversifying your income, you create a safety net that can help you overcome setbacks and continue progressing towards financial freedom.

So, explore different avenues of income, engage in entrepreneurial endeavours, invest wisely, and explore passive income sources. By doing so, you open up possibilities for greater financial security and the ability to pursue your dreams with confidence. Remember, spreading your resources across multiple baskets can be a game-changer in achieving your financial goals.

> *As my nan always reminded me growing up, it is wise to "never put all your eggs in one basket."*

Throughout my financial journey, I have made a variety of investments, some of which have been successful while others have not. It has been a learning experience filled with both good and bad decisions. Taking risks is an essential part of the process, although the level of risk may vary from one investment to another. Along the way, I have gained valuable lessons by being inquisitive, exploring different avenues, and conducting thorough assessments. I have engaged in various investment ventures, including Forex Trading, Stocks, Properties, and entrepreneurship. Each of these avenues has come with its share of wins and losses. Acknowledging the potential for both positive and negative outcomes has been crucial. While some investments have yielded favourable returns, others have taught me valuable lessons. The key is to approach investment opportunities with caution and wisdom. It involves asking pertinent questions, conducting thorough research, and considering potential risks. In doing so, you can make informed decisions that align with your financial goals and risk tolerance. Remember, investing is a continuous learning process. It is essential to adapt and grow, using the knowledge gained from both successes and failures. By embracing the lessons learned along the way, you can further refine your investment strategies and increase your chances of achieving long-term financial success.

In addition to building wealth, it is equally important for you to prioritise financial security. This includes planning for retirement, having adequate insurance coverage, and creating an emergency fund to weather unexpected financial challenges. By proactively managing your financial situations and taking steps to secure your future, you can achieve a sense of peace and confidence in your financial journey. Becoming financially free as a woman is not just about personal success but also about creating a positive impact on future generations. By setting an example of financial independence and breaking through traditional norms, you can then inspire and empower others to take control of their own financial destinies. Through education, mentorship, and empowering conversations, we as women can work together to create a more inclusive and equal financial landscape for all.

If your belief is 'well I am married so I don't need to worry about all of that, my husband's got me.'

Well, this is my take on that, and I know not all of you will agree with me.

Achieving financial freedom as a married woman not only benefits your personal wellbeing but can also contribute to your overall value within your home. When both partners in a relationship have financial independence, it enhances the household's financial stability and security. Having financial freedom allows you to actively contribute to the economic well-being of your family. It enables you to participate in financial decision-making, share the responsibilities of managing finances, and contribute to the achievement of common goals. Moreover, financial independence provides a sense of empowerment and self-confidence, which can positively impact your role within the household.

Financial independence should be seen as an asset in any relationship, regardless of marital status. It fosters mutual respect, equal partnership, and a shared vision for the future. By prioritising your financial well-being, you contribute not only to your own growth and happiness but also to the overall strength and stability of your home. I have never been one to rely solely on my husband or any partner I had prior to my husband, and it was never a pride thing, because I have a relationship with my husband that is built on togetherness, but we also still have what is our own. We are one unit but still embrace our own independence. I am not knocking anyone's choice. I was just never cut out to be a sit-at-home mummy waiting for my husband's paycheque to get what I need to get done. I repeat - this is not a knock on anyone, but I won't apologise for my personal choice and the value I place on myself.

To start on your journey towards financial independence, there are several steps you can take:

1. **Take Control of Your Finances**: Begin by creating a detailed budget and tracking your expenses. This will help

you understand your current financial situation and identify areas where you can cut back or save more.

2. **Increase Your Income**: Look for opportunities to boost your income, such as creating you own business, asking for a raise at work or taking on a side hustle or freelance work. Consider ways to utilise your skills and talents to generate additional streams of income.

3. **Build an Emergency Fund**: Set aside funds for unexpected expenses or emergencies. Having an emergency fund ensures that you won't have to rely on credit cards or loans when faced with unforeseen financial challenges.

4. **Invest in your Skills and Education**: Continuously invest in personal and professional development to enhance your skills and knowledge. This can lead to career advancement or open doors to new opportunities.

5. **Diversify Your Investments**: Begin investing your savings in different assets, such as stocks, bonds, real estate, or mutual funds. Diversifying your portfolio helps to spread risk and potentially increase your returns.

6. **Reduce Debt**: Focus on paying off high-interest debts, such as credit cards or loans. Prioritise paying down debt to free up more of your income for saving and investing.

7. **Seek Professional Advice**: Consider consulting with a financial advisor who can provide valuable guidance and help tailor a financial plan that aligns with your goals and risk tolerance.

Remember, achieving financial independence takes time and consistent effort. Stay disciplined, be patient, and regularly reassess your financial goals to ensure you stay on the right track.

Mastery - **Mastering your skills**

Mastering your skills or talents means achieving a high level of proficiency and expertise in a specific area or field. It surpasses basic competence and involves continuously developing and refining your abilities to become an authority or expert. Mastery represents the pinnacle of proficiency and expertise, marked by comprehensive knowledge, skilful application, continuous growth, recognition, and a devoted pursuit of excellence.

Mastering your skills is crucial for several reasons. Firstly, it boosts your confidence as you improve and attain success, positively impacting both personal and professional aspects of your life. Secondly, it enhances the stability or progression of your business. Additionally, mastery of skills allows for improved performance, increasing productivity and efficiency while reducing effort and stress. Furthermore, it provides a competitive advantage in today's job market, setting you apart as an expert in your field. Lastly, mastering your skills brings personal fulfilment, as it aligns with your passions and contributes to a happier and more satisfying life. In conclusion, continuously developing and refining your skills is key to personal and professional growth, bringing increased value, improved performance, and a sense of achievement.

Mastering your skills and talents can be a valuable way to generate income. When you become an expert in a particular area, you increase your earning potential and open opportunities for freelance work, consulting, or entrepreneurship.

These are some ways you can leverage your skills and talents to make money:

1. **Freelancing**: Offer your services as a freelancer in your field of expertise. This can include anything from writing and graphic design to web development and photography. Freelancing can be done in your spare time while still holding down a full-time job or as a full-time entrepreneur.

2. **Consulting**: If you have specialised knowledge or expertise, consider offering consulting services to businesses or individuals. Consulting can be done in areas such as business strategy, marketing, finance, and technology.

3. **Teaching**: Share your ability and skills by offering classes, coaching or tutoring services. You can develop courses or classes in areas like languages, technology, or even fitness.

4. **Entrepreneurship**: Starting your own business around your skill and talent is another way to make money. This can be in the form of a product or service. For instance, if you have a flair for baking, you can start a catering company or bakery business.

5. **Online Platforms**: Make use of online platforms that connect individuals with experts in specific areas. For example, Udemy.com and Upwork allows instructors to build and sell their own courses to students globally. Also, Fiverr.com is a great platform to sell digital services on such as logo design, video editing, and more.

Remember that earning money from your skills and talents is a process. It takes effort, time, and persistence to generate a stable income. However, by becoming an expert in your field, you increase your earning potential and can create financial freedom through doing what you love.

Momentum

Having momentum as an entrepreneurial woman is of paramount importance for several reasons. Firstly, momentum provides a sense of continuous progress and growth. It fuels motivation, drive, and the determination to overcome obstacles and challenges that may arise along the entrepreneurial journey. This drive enables us to push boundaries, innovate, and explore new opportunities, propelling us towards our goals.

Secondly, momentum fosters confidence and self-belief. When we, as female entrepreneurs, experience consistent success and progress, it reinforces our belief in our abilities and validates our decision to embark on this path. This confidence becomes a powerful asset, empowering us to take risks, make bold decisions, and seize opportunities that may have otherwise seemed daunting.

Furthermore, momentum creates a ripple effect within the entrepreneurial ecosystem. As more women entrepreneurs gain visibility and achieve success, it inspires and encourages others to follow in our footsteps. This momentum not only provides role models and mentors but also helps break down barriers and stereotypes that may discourage other women from pursuing their entrepreneurial dreams, the basis of my writing this book. By fostering an environment that sustains and accelerates momentum as female entrepreneurs, we can tap into the untapped potential and talent to drive a more inclusive and prosperous economy. Having momentum as an entrepreneurial woman is vital for personal growth, confidence, and for attracting support and resources. It also paves the way for wider societal impact, opening doors for more women to pursue their entrepreneurial dreams and contribute to the advancement of economies and communities. By recognising and nurturing this momentum, we create an environment where women entrepreneurs can thrive, succeed, and inspire generations to come.

Staying *Motivated*

Your Why

In this game, one has to stay motivated in order to succeed. There are numerous things that can hit you from the blind side, and at times, it will take all of your strength and courage to keep pushing. Becoming a female entrepreneur is an exhilarating journey filled with numerous challenges and rewards. While there is no denying the tremendous strides we have made in the business world, staying motivated and maintaining a positive mindset is crucial to navigate the ups and downs of entrepreneurship successfully.

I have found that having a strong enough WHY (Purpose) can help keep you motivated. You may get knocked down several time, and getting knocked down at times can be ugly. But guess what? The beauty is in getting back up.

Having a strong "why" as an entrepreneur is paramount to staying motivated and driven on your entrepreneurial journey. Your "why" is the deep-rooted reason behind your decision to become an entrepreneur and the purpose that fuels your actions and decisions. It serves as your guiding light, providing clarity, focus, and a sense of direction. When faced with challenges, setbacks, and obstacles, your "why" acts as a source of inspiration, reminding you of the impact you want to create and the goals you are striving to achieve. It keeps you anchored to your passion, reminding you of the meaningful difference you can make in the world through your entrepreneurial endeavours. Your "why" also provides you with a sense of fulfilment and satisfaction, as it aligns your work with your values and personal mission. By constantly reminding yourself of your "why," you maintain a strong sense of purpose, allowing you to overcome adversity, stay focused, and push through the inevitable rough patches that come with entrepreneurship. It acts as a driving force that empowers you to persevere, innovate, and continue to pursue your goals, even when the path seems uncertain. Your "why" also attracts like-minded individuals to your cause, creating a supportive network and fostering collaboration. Ultimately, having a clear and compelling "why" as an entrepreneur fuels your motivation, enables you to navigate challenges, and propels you towards success and fulfilment. On that note, I would advise you to keep your WHY visible. Let it be something you see daily, especially when navigating through rough waters.

The heart of gratitude

Cultivating gratitude as a powerful tool can have a transformative impact on combating negativity, increasing resilience, and aiding motivation. By focusing on the positive aspects of your life and business, gratitude allows you to shift your mindset from scarcity to abundance. It helps you appreciate the opportunities, successes, and even the simple joys that come with being a woman. This was something that I found so hard to do at one point in my life. Some of you who know me personally may find it hard to believe. I used to be so hard and critical of myself that I never saw or celebrated my wins and was constantly complaining about what did not go well or work. Please do not adopt that mentality. Practice self-compassion. It's amazing how we can show compassion to others but not ourselves, right? Developing self-compassion allows you to navigate setbacks, manage stress, and maintain motivation during challenging times.

You see, here's the thing: I never stopped to embrace the many blessings around me. I thank God the day I started to turn that around and appreciate every single thing - people (both good and bad), situations (both good and bad). Like I spoke about earlier in another chapter, I began to shift my perspective. I was grateful for the bad things because not only did I learn some new tricks that I could share with my ladies, but it also made me more resilient and stronger than I was before the drama happened. Celebrate your achievements, no matter how small. I did not say settle for mediocrity, so please do not hear what I am not saying. I am saying take time to be appreciative of accomplishments and your daily benefits. Recognising and celebrating milestones or achievements helps to boost morale and maintain a positive outlook on the entrepreneurial journey. Celebrating achievements and milestones helps to reinforce motivation and create momentum for future success. Be grateful for another day that you have, another opportunity to work at being the best version of yourself that you can be and make an impact.

By actively practicing gratitude, you train your mind to seek out and acknowledge the goodness around you, even in challenging situations. This shift in perspective not only counteracts negativity but also enhances your resilience by enabling you to reframe setbacks as learning experiences and opportunities for growth. Gratitude also has a profound effect on your overall well-being, as it promotes feelings of joy, contentment, and fulfilment. It reduces stress, increases optimism, and strengthens your emotional and mental well-being. Furthermore, cultivating gratitude fosters a positive work culture, building stronger relationships with team members, customers, and partners. Incorporating gratitude practices, such as journaling, expressing appreciation, or daily reflection, into your entrepreneurial journey can unlock a multitude of benefits, allowing you to navigate challenges with grace, stay motivated, and cultivate a fulfilling and successful entrepreneurial path.

Seeking Support Network

Connecting with fellow female entrepreneurs, mentors, and support groups is not only a valuable avenue for sharing experiences and seeking advice but also a crucial factor in maintaining motivation. By engaging with others in your entrepreneurial community, you can foster a sense of camaraderie and support, which can uplift your spirits during challenging times. Moreover, networking and collaborating with like-minded individuals can generate fresh ideas and opportunities, helping you to stay motivated and inspired. Seeking out role models and mentors, particularly successful female entrepreneurs, can provide invaluable guidance, inspiration, and perspective on your own entrepreneurial journey. Additionally, continuous learning plays a vital role in staying motivated. Actively participating in conferences, workshops, and podcasts, as well as reading relevant books, keeps you up-to-date with industry trends, exposes you to new insights, and ignites your creativity. These activities empower you to continuously evolve, adapt, and stay motivated in your pursuit of entrepreneurial success.

Staying motivated as a female entrepreneur is an ongoing process that requires cultivating a positive mindset, nurturing self-care practices, setting realistic goals, embracing failure, and seeking inspiration from various sources. By implementing the strategies mentioned in this section we as female entrepreneurs can not only maintain our motivation but also unlock our full potential. You can achieve your entrepreneurial dreams and become influential forces in the business world. Remember, success is not a destination; it's a journey fuelled by passion, resilience, and an unwavering commitment to personal and professional growth.

As this chapter comes to an end, I want you to understand that having the ability to have success in all areas of life requires strategy and clear setting of goals for each area of your life that you want to excel in.

I will end with these few tips:

- Break them down into smaller, actionable steps that you can take on a daily basis.
- Consistency and perseverance are key.
- Never underestimate the power of continuous learning and self-improvement.
- Invest in your education and skill development.
- Stay updated with industry trends, attend workshops, and seek out opportunities for growth. The more knowledge and expertise you acquire, the more confident you will become in your abilities.
- Be true to yourself and stay authentic. Do not compare yourself to others or try to live up to societal expectations.
- Celebrate your unique qualities and embrace your individual journey.
- Stay focused on your goals and remember that creating success is a lifelong process.
- Believe in yourself and your capabilities. You are capable of achieving incredible things in all areas of your life.
- Embrace the challenges, put in the hard but smart work, and watch as you blossom into the successful, empowered woman you are meant to be.

Community

facebook.com/TheEikonicWomanCommunity

- *The importance of levelling up*
- *Levelling up as an entrepreneur*

It's time to LEVEL UP!

CHAPTER SIX

It's time to LEVEL UP!

"On a headstone there is the date of birth and the date of death however the real story is what the dash in between says about your time here on earth."

MICHELLE WATSON

Ladies levelling up goes beyond simply achieving success or reaching goals; it is about pursuing your personal and professional goals at the highest level possible, stepping out of your comfort zone, and intelligently pushing yourself in areas that will lead to fulfilment, balance and long-term success. Levelling up involves a mindset shift, where you recognise your own potential and commit to constantly challenging yourself to become the best version of yourself. It requires you to identify your strengths and weaknesses, and then proactively seek opportunities to develop and enhance your skills.

This could mean taking on new projects or responsibilities, seeking out mentors or coaches who can provide guidance and support, or investing in your own personal development through courses, workshops, or self-reflection. Levelling up also involves embracing discomfort and uncertainty, as growth often occurs outside of one's comfort zone. By pushing yourself beyond what is familiar, you open yourself up to new experiences and discover your true capabilities. However, it's important to approach this process intelligently, understanding that levelling up is not about constantly pushing oneself to the point of burnout or sacrificing one's well-being. It's about finding the right balance between ambition and self-care, recognising the importance of setting boundaries and taking care of your physical, mental, and emotional well-being. Ultimately, a woman who is committed to levelling up is one who prioritises her growth, embraces challenges, and pursues fulfilment and long-term happiness in all areas of her life. It is about no longer settling for mediocre or the level you have been for the past few years. I am going to say something now that may be hard hitting but your honesty will determine how you take it. If you look back to the past two years and everything is the same now as it was back then, it is possible you are simply existing; you need to have a serious conversation with yourself. I hope you hear what I am saying and not what I am not! I am not saying that you would need to be rich in two years but there has to be some level of growth, realisation or shift.

You were not born to simply exist; you were born to thrive and excel. You have within you the potential to accomplish greatness, to realise your dreams, and to make an impact in this world. To settle for anything less than that would be to deny yourself the opportunity to unleash your full potential. As you navigate through life, remember that it is okay to aim high, to strive for excellence, and to never settle for mediocrity. Do not let life's challenges or societal expectations dim your light or lower your standards. Embrace your individuality, celebrate your gifts, and pursue your passions fearlessly.

Levelling up as an entrepreneur

Levelling up as an entrepreneur means scaling your business. As an entrepreneur, one of the key goals is to scale your business and take it to new heights. Levelling up involves expanding your operations, reaching new markets, and increasing your impact.

It is an exhilarating journey that requires strategic planning, careful execution, and a mindset geared towards growth. Scaling your business brings numerous benefits. It allows you to tap into new revenue streams, attract more customers, and enhance your brand's visibility. Additionally, it opens doors for partnerships and collaborations that can propel your business forward. By scaling, you create opportunities for yourself and your team to thrive while making a significant impact in your industry.

> *If you look back to the past two years and everything is the same now as it was back then, it is possible you are simply existing.*

To successfully level up as an entrepreneur, it is crucial to develop a solid growth strategy. This involves understanding your target market, analysing industry trends, and identifying opportunities for expansion. You may need to explore new distribution channels, invest in marketing and advertising, or optimise your operations to handle increased demand. Additionally, surrounding yourself with a skilled and dedicated team is essential to supporting your growth journey.

As you strive to scale your business, it is important to remain agile and adaptable. Markets and customer preferences evolve, and it's crucial to stay ahead of the curve. Embrace innovation, constantly seek feedback, and be open to refining your strategies along the way. The ability to embrace change and pivot when necessary will be pivotal in your journey toward entrepreneurial growth success.

So, as you embark on the journey of scaling your business, remember that levelling up is not just about increasing your revenue or expanding your operations. It is about embracing a mindset of growth, seizing opportunities, and leaving a lasting impact. With dedication, strategy, and a passion for what you do, you have the power to take your business to new heights and achieve entrepreneurial greatness. Scaling your business refers to the process of expanding and growing your operations to accommodate increased demand and reach a wider audience. It involves increasing your revenue, customer base, and market presence while maintaining or improving efficiency and profitability.

Here are some key strategies to consider when scaling your business:

Develop a Growth Strategy: Define your vision and set clear growth goals. Assess market opportunities, analyse your target audience, and identify the most effective channels to reach new customers. Create a comprehensive plan that outlines actionable steps to achieve your growth objectives.

Optimise Operations: Streamline your processes and operations to increase efficiency and productivity. Automate repetitive tasks, leverage technology, and invest in systems that can handle higher volumes of work. Regularly review and improve your workflows to ensure smooth scaling.

Building a Strong Team: Surround yourself with talented individuals who are aligned with your vision and can contribute to your business's growth. Delegate responsibilities and empower your team members to take ownership of key areas. Invest in training and development to enhance their skills and capabilities.

Expanding your Market Reach: Identify new markets and segments that align with your target audience. Develop marketing and sales strategies that cater to these markets and leverage different channels, such as social media, collaborations, partnerships, or strategic alliances to increase your brand's visibility and reach.

Enhancing Customer Experience: Prioritise customer satisfaction and retention. Provide exceptional service, listen to customer feedback, and continually improve your offerings based on their needs. Implement CRM systems and other tools to manage and nurture customer relationships effectively.

Securing Adequate Resources: Scaling requires additional resources, whether it's funding, equipment, technology, or human capital. Assess your financial needs and explore funding options like loans, investments, or partnerships. Ensure you have the necessary resources in place to support your growth plans.

Monitoring and Analyse Metrics: Continuously track key performance indicators (KPIs) and gather data to measure your progress and make informed decisions. Monitor sales, customer acquisition costs, customer lifetime value, and other relevant metrics to assess the effectiveness of your scaling efforts.

Adapting to Changing Market Dynamics: Stay agile and adapt to evolving market trends and consumer preferences. Regularly assess your strategies and make adjustments to capitalise on new opportunities or address emerging challenges.

Remember, scaling a business is not a one-size-fits-all approach. It requires careful planning, execution, and constant evaluation. Regularly assess your progress, seek feedback, and be willing to pivot and make necessary adjustments along the way. With the right strategies and a growth mindset, you can successfully scale your business and achieve your long-term objectives.

Let's end by looking at an example of possible steps a coach could take to scale her business.

Scaling a coaching business can involve various strategies and approaches depending on the specific coaching niche and target audience. Here are a few ways of how you can scale a coaching business:

1. **Group Coaching Programs**: Instead of working with clients individually, consider offering group coaching programs. (So, one to many instead of 1:2:1) This allows you to serve multiple clients simultaneously, increasing your reach and revenue. Develop structured programs with predefined curriculum and deliver them through webinars, online courses, or group coaching sessions.

2. **Online Platforms and Courses**: Create and sell online courses or digital products related to your coaching expertise. This allows you to reach a wider audience beyond geographical limitations. You can use platforms like Teachable, Udemy, or Thinkific to host and sell your courses, providing flexibility to clients who prefer self-paced learning.

3. **Train and Certify Coaches**: Develop a training program to certify other coaches in your coaching niche. By training and certifying coaches, you can expand your impact by having graduates deliver coaching services under your brand or umbrella. This allows you to earn income through their coaching fees or certification fees.

4. **Speaking Engagements and Workshops**: Offer speaking engagements and workshops at conferences, events, or within companies. This increases your visibility, establishes you as an expert in your field, and can attract potential coaching clients or corporate coaching opportunities. Market your

speaking services through networking, social media, and professional associations.

5. **Online Membership or Subscription Model**: Create a membership site or subscription model that offers exclusive content, resources, or ongoing coaching support to members. This provides recurring revenue and builds a community of like-minded individuals. You can use platforms like Patreon, Kajabi, Go High Level, or Thinkific to set up and manage a membership site.

6. **Collaborations and Partnerships**: Collaborate with complementary coaches or experts to co-create programs, host joint webinars, or offer bundled services. By leveraging the networks and expertise of others, you can expand your reach and attract a broader client base.

7. **Licensing or Franchising**: If you have developed a unique coaching methodology or program, you can explore licensing or franchising options. This allows others to deliver your coaching services under your brand, following your established model and guidelines.

Remember that scaling a coaching business or any business for that matter requires careful planning, marketing, and ongoing evaluation.

Each coaching business is unique, so tailor your scaling strategies to align with your coaching niche, target audience, and long-term objectives. Remember some of what got you to the position you are now may not be the tools, people or environment that will get you to the next stage, you may have to change a few things like mentor, mindsets and mechanisms in order to advance.

Good luck in scaling your coaching business.

Leave
Your
Mark

CHAPTER SEVEN

Leave Your Mark

"Don't limit yourself. Many people limit themselves to what they think they can do. You can go as far as your mind lets you. What you believe, remember, you can achieve."

MARY KAY ASH

I remember the first serious health scare I had after being diagnosed with AS (Ankylosing Spondylitis) - a word I had to learn to pronounce and had never heard of in my life. I thought my world had ended. I remembered one day being unable to move, screaming in agony as my husband rushed up the stairs. I stood naked, having just come out of the shower, and all I knew and remembered was the last movement of beginning to cream my skin. I was convinced I was paralysed. For two years after, it was a tumult of battles, in and out of the hospital, being told what I had to do or what I could no longer do for the rest of my life (based on their report). Honestly, ladies, I crumbled. I started to see and accept what had been said to me, forgetting God's report and will for my life. The purpose I held so dear seemed to slowly be slipping away.

One day, God showed me a vision. I saw myself walking through a dark tunnel. As I navigated through this tunnel, there were potholes and debris - it was a very rough path. But each section I got through, I would come across a lantern that I could use as a light to see as I walked through the tunnel. The vision then took two folds.

Fold 1: I went through the tunnel and took all the lanterns with me. The more I had, the better I would be able to see and I no longer had any difficulties or experienced any further stumbling. I could see everything clearly. I was so excited and happy when I exited, until I realised that there were other people now coming through the tunnel. They were hitting into things, tripping, falling into the potholes, and getting badly hurt. I felt so guilty because as I looked in my hands, I stood there with all the lanterns. I had left none behind to aid those who would walk through after me.

Fold 2: I went through the tunnel and as I did, I took the first lantern. At each stage I got to where I could take another lantern with me, I left it behind which meant I was going through with only one lantern. Having only one lantern wasn't great - my journey was not as smooth as the first time. Unfortunately, I still bumped into a things, made some bad steps, and even fell a few times. But I was able to get back up. In the end, I made it through the tunnel. But this time, I positioned myself so I could shout and help navigate those who were now coming through. I was not only excited and happy, but I felt fulfilled seeing them exit with a lantern that they were able to use to guide their steps through the rough path of the tunnel.

When this vision ended, and God gave me the full understanding, oh wow, it spoke volumes to me.

The tunnel was me going through life. I could choose to be angry and bitter because I wanted to have the easy life - you know, the life we always desire, the 'soft life' where we don't stumble or hit roadblocks and debris, the place where we go into the 'why me, Lord!' 'Why me again?' 'Why do I have to be the one going through this?' I realised that I could continuously grumble and wallow in self-pity and choose to be selfish with the lessons I have learnt going through life. I could take them to the grave with me, having not made any impact or left anything behind to help others who would be walking a similar path that I have trod.

Or

I could choose to be a part of the light, leaving something behind to help others navigate, shed some light on those potholes so that other ladies like yourself can know where they are, let you hear my lessons of life, and be able to learn, grow, and succeed even better than I did and pave the way for future generations.

Here's the thing, ladies. Our life's lessons that we experience are not just ours. As we go through the tunnel of life, we have the option to leave this earth with all the knowledge, experience, and wisdom we have gathered along the way, or we can choose to utilise them, share, and make them available for others on their journey. Many coaches and mentors are not necessarily successful because they are Ph.D. holders but more so because they are experience holders and life lesson learners. When we encounter challenges or setbacks, we gain valuable insights that can serve as guideposts for our future journey. Embracing the dynamism of our experiences allows us to pave the way for personal growth, learn from our mistakes, and share our wisdom with others.

So, recognising the ever-changing nature of our lives means embracing the lessons we gain from our experiences and using them to navigate our paths with greater wisdom, resilience, and the ability to uplift and support others. By embracing the dynamic nature of our lives, we can let go of the pressure to have everything figured out and allow ourselves to explore, experiment, and adapt. And through those adaptations, we gain the valuable nuggets that can be then passed on.

My dear Eikonic Woman, you have within you the power to leave an indelible mark on this world. Your unique talents, dreams, and experiences make you a force to be reckoned with. It's time to unleash that inner fire and embrace the limitless possibilities that lie ahead. Leaving your mark doesn't mean conforming or following the crowd. It's about tapping into your authentic self, standing tall in your truth, and sharing your unique voice with the world. It's about embracing your passions, pursuing your ambitions, and making a difference in your own special way. Don't be afraid to dream big, my fellow trailblazer. Set audacious goals that ignite your soul and propel you towards greatness. Be fearless in the pursuit of your dreams, knowing that every step you take brings you closer to leaving your mark. Remember, setbacks and challenges are merely opportunities in disguise - they are stepping stones towards growth and resilience. But leaving your mark isn't just about personal achievement; it's about creating a ripple effect that inspires and uplifts others so that they, in return, can also then lift others. Share your experiences, both the triumphs and the trials, for they hold the power to touch the lives of others. Your journey, your wisdom, and your unique perspective can spark a fire within someone else, empowering them to embrace their own potential and embark on their own path of success.

After having that vision, I shared with you earlier, it reignited a fire within me, to not give up, it realigned me with my WHY and gave me the drive to keep pushing and to start again after two years. I read Titus 2:3-5 and it was the confirmation I needed to set the wheels back in motion.

Older women likewise are to be reverent in behaviour,
not slanderers or slaves to much wine. They are to teach
what is good, and so train the young women to love
their husbands and children, to be self-controlled, pure,
working at home, kind, and submissive to their own
husbands, that the word of God may not be reviled.

This is what got laid on my heart

Women Raising Women: The Titus 2 woman

Ah, the Titus 2 Woman - a beacon of wisdom, grace, and strength. She holds a special place in my heart and is the model I choose to follow, for she embodies the essence of what it means to be an Eikonic Woman. So, my dear Eikonic Woman, let us delve into the concept of the Titus 2 Woman and the powerful lessons she imparts. I drew inspiration from the biblical book of Titus in creating the Eikonic woman, which beautifully emphasises the importance of mentorship and guiding others towards a life of excellence. She is a woman who understands the power of her experiences and lessons learned and is eager to share them with the generations that follow.

In her nurturing and authentic demeanour, the Titus 2 Woman holds the key to fostering a culture of learning, growth, and empowerment. She understands that collective success is not achieved in isolation, but through the power of mentorship and support. She embraces the responsibility to nurture and guide those around her, using her own journey as a foundation for imparting wisdom. The Titus 2 Woman recognises the importance of modelling resilience, integrity, and faith. Through her actions, she teaches others to face challenges with grace, to walk in truth, and to hold firm to their beliefs. In doing so, she becomes a living example of the transformative power of character and conviction.

But let us not forget the reciprocal nature of the Titus 2 relationship. While the mentor imparts wisdom, the mentee brings fresh perspective, enthusiasm, and a hunger for knowledge. The Titus 2 Woman understands that growth is a two-way street, where both mentor and mentee learn and evolve together. In this beautiful symbiosis, a powerful bond is formed, cultivating a flourishing community of shared success.

So, my dear Eikonic Woman, whether you find yourself as the mentor or the mentee, I encourage you to embrace the principles of the Titus 2 Woman. Tap into the power of mentorship and seek guidance from those who have walked the path before you. As a mentor, share your experiences, uplift others, and be a beacon of hope and inspiration. As a mentee, absorb the wisdom shared, ask questions, and honour the lessons of those who have blazed the trail before you. In embracing the spirit of the Titus 2 Woman, we create a legacy of empowerment, growth, and collective success for generations to come. So, my fellow Eikonic Woman, let us continue to nurture and support one another, for in doing so, we embody the true essence of an Eikonic Woman - empowering, authentic, and forever uplifting.

So, where and when you can teach, learn, support, and allow the power of collaboration to unfold.

In an era defined by empowerment and equality, a powerful movement is women supporting women and collaborating. This collective force is breaking down barriers, inspiring change, and redefining what it means to succeed. When women come together, they create a vibrant and unstoppable energy that propels us all towards greatness.

Reminders

There is Strength in Collaboration:

In a world that sometimes pits women against each other, collaboration emerges as a refreshing antidote. When women join forces and combine their skills, knowledge, and resources, the possibilities become limitless. Collaboration fosters innovation, ignites creativity, and sparks a synergy that propels us beyond individual limitations. Together, we become stronger, wiser, and capable of achieving remarkable feats. By leveraging each other's strengths, we create a web of support and expertise, helping one another reach new heights of success.

Breaks Down Barriers:

When women come together, they possess the collective power to shatter societal barriers and dismantle long-standing prejudices. By supporting and uplifting one another, we challenge the status quo and pave the way for future generations. When we collaborate, we create a culture of inclusivity, where the diversity of our experiences and perspectives is celebrated. By standing united, we make it clear that every woman's voice deserves to be heard, respected, and valued. Together, we challenge the limitations placed upon us and create a world that knows no boundaries.

Mentorship and Empowering Others:

One of the most remarkable aspects of women supporting women is the transformative power of mentorship. As successful women, it is our duty to uplift and empower those who are on their own journey towards greatness. By sharing our knowledge, experiences, and wisdom, we light the way for others, encouraging them to dream bigger and reach higher. Mentorship creates a ripple effect, as empowered women go on to empower others, creating a powerful cycle of success and growth. We have the opportunity to change lives, inspire future leaders, and create a legacy that extends far beyond ourselves.

The Sisterhood Connection:

When women support women, a profound sense of sisterhood emerges, COMMUNITY! We become a tribe connected by shared experiences, passions, and ambitions. This sisterhood offers solace, understanding, and unwavering support. Together, we form a community that nurtures personal and professional growth, where vulnerability is embraced, and victories are celebrated fiercely. In this safe and nurturing space, we find the strength to overcome challenges, persevere through adversity, and stand resolute in our pursuit of our dreams.

The power of women collaboration and women supporting women is awe-inspiring. Together, we unleash our full potential, breaking down barriers, inspiring change, and creating a world where every woman can thrive. As we uplift one another, we create a collective force of success that cannot be denied. Let us continue to celebrate each other's achievements, amplify each other's voices, and encourage one another to reach higher. For in the journey of shared success, we find our true power.

Together, we are stronger.

Surround yourself with a tribe of like-minded individuals who believe in your vision and support your dreams. Seek out mentors who have forged their own paths and are willing to guide you. And, in turn, be a mentor yourself, shining a light for others as they navigate their own journeys. So, as you go forth and aim to leave your mark, remember that you are not alone. You are a part of a vibrant community of ambitious women, each carving her own unique path to success. Embrace the power of collective growth, celebrate the achievements of your fellow sisters, and uplift one another on this incredible journey.

I can't wait to see the mark you leave on this world. Your passions, your dreams, and your voice are what make you truly extraordinary. Embrace them, share them, and watch as you inspire and empower others along the way. Keep shining, keep striving, and keep leaving your mark - the world is waiting for you!

Acknowledgments

First and foremost, I want to express my deepest gratitude to God, who has given me the grace not only to write this book but also to bless me with a journey that I hope will be a blessing to others.

To my rock of a husband, Al, and my wonderful children, Santana, Rashaun, and Alisha, I love you all with all my heart. You have been my biggest reason for why I've kept going, even during times when I wanted to give up. I also want to thank my family and friends who have been a source of strength and support. Your love and encouragement have meant everything to me.

I want to give a special shout-out to my church family, ARC Global, and my Elders Omar & Rhona Tackie, Peter & Aunty Caris, Colin & Sabrina, Daniel & Lydia, for their spiritual covering, prayers, and teachings. To my fellow Deacons, Tayo, Maggie, and Lewis, thank you for being my spiritual support and my shoulders to lean on. And to my ARC 2.0 clan, thank you for embracing me as your own 'mummy Mich.' I pray that God will continue to pour out blessings upon you, as you continue to pour out your love and trust into me.

A special thanks to my prayer partner, cousin, and confidant, Staceyann. Your unwavering love, care, and support have meant everything to me. Thank you for being my cheerleader, encourager, prayer warrior, and friend. I am grateful to God for you, and I pray that He continues to bless you as you continue to excel as an Eikonic woman.

To my first-ever Eikonic Women, you know who you are. I want to express my love for you all. You will always have a special place in my heart.

And finally, to everyone who made this book possible, Kennes and Stephan, your phenomenal work speaks for itself. Thank you for all your hard work and dedication in helping to bring my vision to life.

There are many more I could mention but the list would go on forever, I thank God for the people he has placed in my life as mentors and mentees, individuals who have seen me as a mother in their life and values my advice and guidance. Thank you for loving and trusting me.

All I can say is God is good x

Congratulations!

On completing the book all the way to the end. As a way of celebrating your commitment, I would like to gift you a freebie for staying committed to the end. Scan the barcode to immediately claim your gift.

Scan me

www.michellewatson.biz/training

About The Author

Michelle Watson is an accomplished international speaker, mentor, book and business accelerator coach, bestselling author, podcast host, Deacon, wife, and mother. She has earned multiple prestigious awards throughout her career. Michelle is not only a survivor of domestic abuse, suicidal tendencies, and depression but also a beacon of hope for others facing similar challenges. Her powerful storytelling and impactful speeches have graced  renowned platforms such as the Women's Economic Forum and the National Achievers Congress UK. Michelle's expertise has garnered attention from various media outlets, including Sky TV, Harold Radio, Womelle Magazine, and the Harvard Business Magazine. She is the visionary behind Breakfree Forever Consultancy LTD, a company dedicated to assisting entrepreneurs, speakers, and businesses in sharing their stories and expertise with the world. Her services help clients increase their visibility, influence, and sales while leaving a lasting legacy.

Michelle has made a massive impact on personal growth and her transformational work is unparalleled. Through her expertise in personal development, mentoring, writing, and public speaking, she has guided countless individuals worldwide to elevate themselves from ordinary to extraordinary. Her dedication to life transformation, motivation, vision creation, and financial growth has earned her numerous accolades and affiliations. Michelle's true passion lies in empowering individuals, families, entrepreneurs, and organizations to reach their personal, financial, and entrepreneurial aspirations. As a highly sought-after speaker, she has collaborated with influential individuals to accelerate transformation and make a lasting impact. Michelle's authorship includes four impactful books, including the bestseller "Overcome & Rise Above – How to Turn the Downside of Your Challenges into The Upside of Renewing Your Life," and "Rise Above & Believe It's Do or Lie – How to Get Rid of Excuses & Create the Life You Desire." Notably, she has also co-written three other powerful books, such as "Authority – How to Write Your Book & Use It as A Marketing Tool for Your Business, Your Book & Beyond.

Spoken on stages/organisations such as

- The Women Economic Forum
- National Achievers Congress
- Power to Achieve (Amsterdam)
- Events for Champions (Thailand)
- Professional Speakers Academy (Dubai)
- The National Commercial Bank (Jamaica)

Featured On/In

- Sky TV,
- Harold Hill radio,
- Womelle Magazine
- Harvard Business Review Magazine
- London Live TV
- The Digging Deep Show

- Power Xtra Radio
- Stand Out Woman Radio
- Oasis Universal Radio

Awards / Honours Received

- Letter of commendation from Her Majesty the Queen (2017)
- Mentor of The Year (2018)
- Performance Coach of The Year (2020)
- Speaker of The Year (2017)
- Best Opening to a Presentation (2016)
- Global Authors Award (2018)
- Women Appreciating Women Awards (2020)
- Global Women Awards (2022)

Author

- Overcome & Rise Above (Bestseller)
- Rise Above & Believe
- Authority
- The Eikonic Woman
- Your Book & Beyond

Co-Authored

- Ordinary Women doing Extraordinary Things
- Les Brown Changed My Life
- Stories of Truth

Most requested speaking and training topics

- Developing healthy boundaries & a strong sense of self worth
- Influential Leadership

- Resilience & The Confidence Principle
- Mental Health & Suicidal Prevention
- Creating Content That Sells
- Developing The Mindset for Success
- Write to Become an Authority
- Domestic Abuse & Women Empowerment
- Teamwork in The Workplace
- How to Turn the Downside of Challenges to The Upside of Renewing Your Life
- Turn your passion into profit
- The Power of Storytelling

Would You Like To Work With Me?

Services

www.michellewatson.biz/services/

What I Do

Harness Michelle Watson's strategic acumen for crafting your life's vision. Her targeted guidance facilitates clear goal-setting and actionable plans, ensuring lasting success and fulfillment.

Personal Empowerment

Embark on a journey of self-discovery with Michelle Watson's empowerment coaching. Transform your life by breaking through personal barriers and embracing your full potential.

Mentorship & Coaching

Receive personalized guidance and support from an experienced mentor. Michelle's coaching programs are designed to guide you in achieving your personal and professional goals.

Strategy & Growth

Elevate your business with strategic planning and growth services. From idea to execution, Michelle's expertise will help you scale your business and increase your market presence.

Leadership Development

Step into your power with leadership training that inspires influence and impact. Develop the skills necessary to lead with confidence and integrity in any arena. Michelle can help.

Michelle's *Books*

Co-Authored *Books*

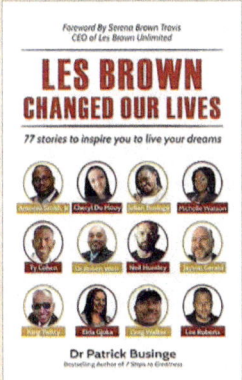

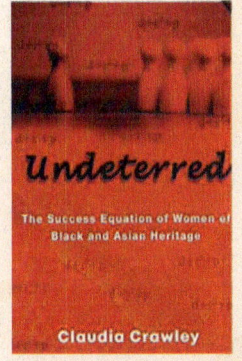

Printed in Great Britain
by Amazon

48077289R00126